SECOND EDITION

TOP NOTCH

English for Today's World

1

Joan Saslow • Allen Ascher

With *Top Notch Pop Songs and Karaoke*
by Rob Morsberger

PEARSON
Longman

Top Notch: English for Today's World 1, Second Edition

Pearson Education, 10 Bank Street, White Plains, NY 10606

Staff credits: The people who made up the *Top Notch 1* team—representing editorial, design, production, and manufacturing—are Rhea Banker, Elizabeth Carlson, Aerin Csigay, Dave Dickey, Warren Fischbach, Aliza Greenblatt, Ray Keating, Mike Kemper, Barbara Sabella, and Martin Yu.

Cover design: Rhea Banker
Cover photo: Sprint/Corbis
Text design: Elizabeth Carlson
Text composition: Quarasan!
Text font: 9/10 Stone Sans

Library of Congress Cataloging-in-Publication Data

Saslow, Joan M.
  Top notch : English for today's world / Joan Saslow, Allen Ascher ; with Top Notch pop songs and Karaoke by
  Rob Morsberger. — 2nd ed.
     p. cm.
  ISBN 0-13-246988-X (set) — ISBN 0-13-247038-1 (v. 1) — ISBN 0-13-247048-9 (v. 2) — ISBN 0-13-247027-6
  (v. 3) 1. English language — Textbooks for foreign speakers. 2. English language — Problems, exercises, etc.
  I. Ascher, Allen. II. Title.
  PE1128.S2757 2011
  428.2'4 — dc22

                                   2010019162

Photo credits: All original photography by Michal Heron and Sharon Hoogstraten. Page 2 (background) Shutterstock.com, (top left) Michael S. Yamashita/Corbis, (middle) michaeljung/Shutterstock, (right) Peter Turnley/Corbis, (bottom left) Ariel Skelley/Corbis; p. 3 (bottom left) Bryan Bedder/Getty Images, (bottom right) LAN/Corbis; p. 5 (top) Shutterstock.com; p. 6 (left) Jason Merritt/Getty Images; p. 7 (top left) AP Images/Chris Pizzello, (top right) Kevin Mazur/Getty Images, (bottom) AP Images/Stephen Chernin; p. 9 (top left) Shutterstock.com, (top right) Shutterstock.com, (middle left) Shutterstock.com, (middle right) Shutterstock.com; p. 11 (right) Shutterstock.com; p. 12 Shutterstock.com; p. 13 (top right) AP Images/Diane Bondareff, (middle) iStockphoto.com, (bottom) Shutterstock.com, (bottom background) Shutterstock.com; p. 15 Dorling Kindersley; p. 21 (top middle) Peter Klaunzer/Corbis, (top right) Jo Hale/Getty Images, (bottom middle) Scala/Art Resource, NY, (bottom right) Vincent West/Reuters/Corbis; p. 22 (top left) Shutterstock.com; p. 25 (background) Shutterstock.com; p. 26 (grandparents) Lindy Powers/Index Stock Imagery, (Linda) Shutterstock.com, (uncle, aunt, cousins) Getty Images, (parents) Ryan McVay/Getty Images, (mother-in-law) Ron Chapple/Getty Images, (father-in-law) James Darell/Getty Images, (sister-in-law, brother, nephew, niece) Royalty-Free/Corbis, (sister) Cleve Bryant/PhotoEdit, (children) Shutterstock.com, (brother-in-law) Bill Cannon/Getty Images; p. 30 (top left) Jerome Tisne/Getty Images, (top middle) Mel Yates/Getty Images, (top right) Astock/Corbis, (bottom left) Andersen Ross/Jupiterimages, (bottom middle) Terry Vine/Corbis, (bottom right) Photos.com; p. 37 (background) Shutterstock.com, (Enrique) Alexander Tamargo/Getty Images, (Ronna) Europa Press/Gamma/eyedea/picturedesk.com, (Dr. Julio) Europa Press/Gamma/eyedea/picturedesk.com, (Miranda) Torra Terry/Gamma/eyedea/picturedesk.com, (Julio) Robert Duyos/AFP/Getty Images, (Isabel P.) Carlos Alvarez/Getty Images, (Guillermo) Europa Press/Gamma/eyedea/picturedesk.com, (Victoria) Europa Press/Gamma/eyedea/picturedesk.com, (Cristina) Europa Press/Gamma/eyedea/picturedesk.com, (Rodrigo) Europa Press/Gamma/eyedea/picturedesk.com, (Miguel) Europa Press/Gamma/eyedea/picturedesk.com, (Isabel) Alexander Tamargo/Getty Images, (Julio) Stephane Cardinale/People Avenue/Corbis, (Enrique) Alexander Tamargo/Getty Images; p. 38 (top left) Shutterstock.com, (potato soup) Jupiterimages/Getty Images, (fried squid) iStockphoto.com, (tomato onion) Image Source/PictureQuest-Royalty Free, (fish) Colin Cooke/Getty Images, (chicken) Tom Vano/Jupiterimages, (cake) Francisco Cruz/SuperStock; p. 41 (sandwich) iStockphoto.com; p. 46 (top right) C Squared Studios/Getty Images, (left) Shutterstock.com, (middle) Amy Etra/PhotoEdit Inc., (right) Shutterstock.com; p. 49 (background) iStockphoto.com, (1) Comstock Images/Getty Images, (2) Jacobs Stock Photography/Getty Images, (3) Jochen Sand/Getty Images, (4) iStockphoto.com, (salad) Shutterstock.com, (pasta) Shutterstock.com, (fish) Dorling Kindersley, (shrimp) Dorling Kindersley; p. 50 (laptop) Shutterstock.com, (desktop) Shutterstock.com, (earphone) Shutterstock.com, (gps) Shutterstock.com, (dvd) iStockphoto.com, (flash) Shutterstock.com, (camera) courtesy Canon USA, (headphones) Shutterstock.com, (earbuds) Shutterstock.com, (projector) iStockphoto.com, (mp3) iStockphoto.com, (camcorder) Shutterstock.com, (speakers) Logitech, Inc.; p. 82 (tv) Shutterstock.com; p. 53 (smart) Shutterstock.com, (cell) Nokia, (scanner) iStockphoto.com, (photocopier) Getty Images, (fax) EyeWire Collection/Getty Images; p. 54 (top right) Anthony Meshkinyar/Getty Images, (2) Silver Burdett Ginn, (3) Melba Photo Agency/PunchStock, (4) Shutterstock.com, (5) Dorling Kindersley, (6) Shutterstock.com, (7) Shutterstock.com, (8) Piotr Maslej, (10) Shutterstock.com, (11) Will Crocker/Getty Images, (13) iStockphoto.com, (14) Peter Holmes/Photolibrary, (16) Photos.com, (17) Shutterstock.com; p. 56 (top) Shutterstock.com, (middle) Shutterstock.com, (right) Shutterstock.com; p. 61 (background) Mikael Dubois/Getty Images, (1) iStockphoto.com and Shutterstock.com, (2) Jim Corwin/Getty Images, (middle) iStockphoto.com, (3) PhotosIndia/Getty Images and Shutterstock.com, (4 left) Shutterstock.com, (4 middle) Hitoshi Nishimura/Getty Images, (4 right) Shutterstock.com; p. 62 (top) PhotoDisc/Getty Images, (bottom) Shutterstock.com; p. 63 (background) iStockphoto.com, (top right) Radius Images/Alamy; p. 65 (bottom) Shutterstock.com; p. 66 (park) Rudi Von Briel/PhotoEdit, Inc., (gym) David Sacks/Getty Images, (track) Tom Carter/PhotoEdit, Inc., (pool) Pat Lanza/Bruce Coleman Inc., (field) Sergio Piumatti, (course) Dorling Kindersley, (court) R.W. Jones/Corbis; p. 70 (top right) Handout/Getty Images, (left) Bob Daemmrich/Corbis (bottom right) Noah Hamilton; p. 74 (London) Shutterstock.com, (Paris) Shutterstock.com, (Rome) Louis A. Goldman/Photo Researchers, Inc., (Vienna) Javier Larrea/Photolibrary, (Copenhagen) Dreamstime.com, (boat) Shutterstock.com, (windsurf) Shutterstock.com, (snorkel) Bill Varie/Corbis; p. 75 (bottom) Shutterstock.com; p. 76 (background) iStockphoto.com; p. 77 iStockphoto.com; p. 78 Shutterstock.com; p. 79 (Perth) Dorling Kindersley, (Egypt) Shutterstock.com, (New York) Shutterstock.com, (Buenos) Imagebroker/Alamy; p. 80 (left) Gabe Rogel/Getty Images, (middle) Luca Tettoni/Corbis, (right) HFHI/David Snyder; p. 81 (left) Shutterstock.com, (middle right) Shutterstock.com, (right) Shutterstock.com; p. 85 (background) Shutterstock.com; p. 86 (jackets) Dorling Kindersley, (sweaters) Shutterstock.com, (boxers) Comstock Royalty Free Division, (bras) Shutterstock.com, (purses) Dorling Kindersley, (belts) Richard Megna/Fundamental Photographs, (bathrobes) Comstock Royalty Free Division, (shoes) Siede Preis/Getty Images; p. 89 (top left) Shutterstock.com, (top right) Shutterstock.com; p. 94 (travelin) Shutterstock.com, (jillian) Shutterstock.com, (tall) Shutterstock.com, (middle right) LOOK Die Bildagentur der Fotografen GmbH/Alamy; p. 95 Shutterstock.com; p. 98 Shutterstock.com; p. 99 (background left) iStockphoto.com, (background middle) Shutterstock.com, (background right) Shutterstock.com; p. 104 Shutterstock.com; p. 105 (top) Mike Powell/Getty Images, (bottom) Gogo Images/Photolibrary; p. 106 Shutterstock.com; p. 110 (left) iStockphoto.com, (middle) Shutterstock.com, (right) Shutterstock.com; p. 115 (bowls) Shutterstock.com, (vase) Photos.com, (sunglasses) Shutterstock.com, (hat) Dorling Kindersley/Getty Images, (sweater) iStockphoto.com; p. 116 (left) Jamie Grill/Photolibrary, (right) Joshua Ets-Hokin/Photolibrary; p. 117 (left) Shutterstock.com, (middle right) Shutterstock.com, (right) Shutterstock.com; p. 118 (middle) Shutterstock.com, (bottom) Shutterstock.com; p. 119 Shutterstock.com.

Illustration credits: Kenneth Batelman, pp. 40, 88, 92, 93, 100, 107; Rich Burlew, p. 62; John Ceballos, pp. 85, 109; Bob Doucet, pp. 25, 97; Scott Fray, p. 47; Marty Harris, p.77; Michael A. Hill, p. 19; Brian Hughes, pp. 53, 106 (center), 113; Jim Kopp, p. 104; Poul Lange, p. 41; Adam Larkum, p. 73; Pat Lewis, p. 28; Andy Meyer, pp. 8, 57, 106 (top); Sandy Nichols, pp. 24, 80, 102; Janet Norquist, p.18; Dusan Petricic, pp. 17, 42, 43, 82, 83, 118; Phil Scheuer, p. 21(top), 58; Robert Schoolcraft, p. 121; Steven Stankiewicz, p. 20; Anna Veltfort, p. 21(bottom), 59; XNR Productions, pp. 74, 75, 106 (bottom).

Printed in the United States of America

ISBN 10: 0-13-814083-9
ISBN 13: 978-0-13814083-0
13 14 15 – V082 – 17 16 15 14

ISBN 10: 0-13-247038-1 (with MyEnglishLab)
ISBN 13: 978-0-13-247038-4 (with MyEnglishLab)
7 8 9 10 – V082 – 17 16 15 14

About the Authors

Joan Saslow

Joan Saslow has taught in a variety of programs in South America and the United States. She is author of a number of multi-level integrated-skills courses for adults and young adults: *Ready to Go: Language, Lifeskills, and Civics; Workplace Plus: Living and Working in English;* and of *Literacy Plus.* She is also author of *English in Context: Reading Comprehension for Science and Technology.* Ms. Saslow was the series director of *True Colors* and *True Voices.* She participates in the English Language Specialist Program in the U.S. Department of State's Bureau of Educational and Cultural Affairs.

Allen Ascher

Allen Ascher has been a teacher and a teacher trainer in China and the United States and taught in the TESOL Certificate Program at the New School in New York. He was also academic director of the International English Language Institute at Hunter College. Mr. Ascher is author of the "Teaching Speaking" module of *Teacher Development Interactive,* an online multimedia teacher-training program, and of *Think about Editing: A Grammar Editing Guide for ESL.*

Both Ms. Saslow and Mr. Ascher are frequent and popular speakers at professional conferences and international gatherings of EFL and ESL teachers.

Authors' Acknowledgments

The authors are indebted to these reviewers who provided extensive and detailed feedback and suggestions for the second edition of *Top Notch* as well as the hundreds of teachers who participated in surveys and focus groups.

Manuel Aguilar Díaz, El Cultural Trujillo, Peru • **Manal Al Jordi,** Expression Training Company, Kuwait • **José Luis Ames Portocarrero,** El Cultural Arequipa, Peru • **Vanessa de Andrade,** CCBEU Inter Americano, Curitiba, Brazil • **Rossana Aragón Castro,** ICPNA Cusco, Peru • **Jennifer Ballesteros,** Universidad del Valle de México, Campus Tlalpan, Mexico City, Mexico • **Brad Bawtinheimer,** PROULEX, Guadalajara, Mexico • **Carolina Bermeo,** Universidad Central, Bogotá, Colombia • **Zulma Buitrago,** Universidad Pedagógica Nacional, Bogotá, Colombia • **Fabiola R. Cabello,** Idiomas Católica, Lima, Peru • **Emma Campo Collante,** Universidad Central Bogotá, Colombia • **Viviane de Cássia Santos Carlini,** Spectrum Line, Pouso Alegre, Brazil • **Fanny Castelo,** ICPNA Cusco, Peru • **José Luis Castro Moreno,** Universidad de León, Mexico • **Mei Chia-Hong,** Southern Taiwan University (STUT), Taiwan • **Guven Ciftci,** Faith University, Turkey • **Freddy Correa Montenegro,** Centro Colombo Americano, Cali, Colombia • **Alicia Craman de Carmand,** Idiomas Católica, Lima, Peru • **Jesús G. Díaz Osío,** Florida National College, Miami, USA • **Ruth Domínguez,** Universidad Central Bogotá, Colombia • **Roxana Echave,** El Cultural Arequipa, Peru • **Angélica Escobar Chávez,** Universidad de León, Mexico • **John Fieldeldy,** College of Engineering, Nihon University, Aizuwakamatsu-shi, Japan • **Herlinda Flores,** Centro de Idiomas Universidad Veracruzana, Mexico • **Claudia Franco,** Universidad Pedagógica Nacional, Colombia • **Andrea Fredricks,** Embassy CES, San Francisco, USA • **Chen-Chen Fu,** National Kaoshiung First Science Technology University, Taiwan • **María Irma Gallegos Peláez,** Universidad del Valle de México, Mexico City, Mexico • **Carolina García Carbajal,** El Cultural Arequipa, Peru • **Claudia Gavancho Terrazas,** ICPNA Cusco, Peru • **Adriana Gómez,** Centro Colombo Americano, Bogotá, Colombia • **Raphaël Goossens,** ICPNA Cusco, Peru • **Carlo Granados,** Universidad Central, Bogotá, Colombia • **Ralph Grayson,** Idiomas Católica, Lima, Peru • **Murat Gultekin,** Fatih University, Turkey • **Monika Hennessey,** ICPNA Chiclayo, Peru • **Lidia Hernández Medina,** Universidad del Valle de México, Mexico City, Mexico • **Jesse Huang,** National Central University, Taiwan • **Eric Charles Jones,** Seoul University of Technology, South Korea • **Jun-Chen Kuo,** Tajen University, Taiwan • **Susan Krieger,** Embassy CES, San Francisco, USA • **Robert Labelle,** Centre for Training and Development, Dawson College, Canada • **Erin Lemaistre,** Chung-Ang University, South Korea • **Eleanor S. Leu,** Soochow University, Taiwan • **Yihui Li (Stella Li),** Fooyin University, Taiwan • **Chin-Fan Lin,** Shih Hsin University, Taiwan • **Linda Lin,** Tatung Institute of Technology, Taiwan • **Kristen Lindblom,** Embassy CES, San Francisco, USA • **Ricardo López,** PROULEX, Guadalajara, Mexico • **Neil Macleod,** Kansai Gaidai University, Osaka, Japan • **Robyn McMurray,** Pusan National University, South Korea • **Paula Medina,** London Language Institute, Canada • **María Teresa Meléndez de Elorreaga,** ICPNA Chiclayo, Peru • **Sandra Cecilia Mora Espejo,** Universidad del Valle de México, Campus Tlalpan, Mexico City, Mexico • **Ricardo Nausa,** Centro Colombo Americano, Bogotá, Colombia • **Tim Newfields,** Tokyo University Faculty of Economics, Tokyo, Japan • **Mónica Nomberto,** ICPNA Chiclayo, Peru • **Scarlett Ostojic,** Idiomas Católica, Lima, Peru • **Ana Cristina Ochoa,** CCBEU Inter Americano, Curitiba, Brazil • **Doralba Pérez,** Universidad Pedagógica Nacional, Bogotá, Colombia • **David Perez Montalvo,** ICPNA Cusco, Peru • **Wahrena Elizabeth Pfeister,** University of Suwon, South Korea • **Wayne Allen Pfeister,** University of Suwon, South Korea • **Cecilia Ponce de León,** ICPNA Cusco, Peru • **Andrea Rebonato,** CCBEU Inter Americano, Curitiba, Brazil • **Elizabeth Rodríguez López,** El Cultural Trujillo, Peru • **Olga Rodríguez Romero,** El Cultural Trujillo, Peru • **Timothy Samuelson,** BridgeEnglish, Denver, USA • **Enrique Sánchez Guzmán,** PROULEX, Guadalajara, Mexico • **Letícia Santos,** ICBEU Ibiá, Brazil • **Lyndsay Shaeffer,** Embassy CES, San Francisco, USA • **John Eric Sherman,** Hong Ik University, South Korea • **João Vitor Soares,** NACC, São Paulo, Brazil • **Elena Sudakova,** English Language Center, Kiev, Ukraine • **Richard Swingle,** Kansai Gaidai College, Osaka, Japan • **Sandrine Ting,** St. John's University, Taiwan • **Shu-Ping Tsai,** Fooyin University, Taiwan • **José Luis Urbina Hurtado,** Universidad de León, Mexico • **Monica Urteaga,** Idiomas Católica, Lima, Peru • **Juan Carlos Villafuerte,** ICPNA Cusco, Peru • **Dr. Wen-hsien Yang,** National Kaohsiung Hospitality College, Kaohsiung, Taiwan • **Holger Zamora,** ICPNA Cusco, Peru.

Learning Objectives

Top Notch 1 learning objectives are designed for false beginners. They offer a rigorous review and an expansion of key beginning concepts as well as a wealth of new and challenging material.

Unit	Communication Goals	Vocabulary	Grammar
1 **Getting Acquainted** page 2	• Meet someone new • Identify and describe people • Provide personal information • Introduce someone to a group	• Usage of formal titles • Positive adjectives to describe people • Personal information • Countries and nationalities	• Information questions with <u>be</u> (review and common errors) • Modification with adjectives (review) • <u>Yes</u> / <u>no</u> questions and short answers with <u>be</u> (review) **GRAMMAR BOOSTER** • <u>Be</u>: usage and form (review) • <u>Be</u>: common errors • Possessive nouns and adjectives (review)
2 **Going Out** page 14	• Accept or decline an invitation • Express locations and give directions • Make plans to see an event • Talk about musical tastes	• Music genres • Entertainment and cultural events • Locations and directions	• Prepositions of time and place • Questions with <u>When</u>, <u>What time</u>, and <u>Where</u> (review) **GRAMMAR BOOSTER** • Prepositions of time and place: usage

3 **The Extended Family** page 26	• Report news about relationships
	• Describe extended families
	• Compare people
	• Discuss family cultural traditions
		• Extended family relationships
		• Marital status
		• Relatives by marriage
		• Describing similarities and differences
			• The simple present tense (review):
			  ○ Affirmative and negative statements
			  ○ <u>Yes</u> / <u>no</u> questions
			  ○ Information questions
			  ○ Common errors
			
			GRAMMAR BOOSTER
			• The simple present tense:
			  ○ Usage, form, common errors
			  ○ Questions with <u>Who</u>

4 **Food and Restaurants** page 38	• Ask for a restaurant recommendation • Order from a menu • Speak to a server and pay for a meal • Discuss food and health	• Parts of a meal • Categories of food and drink • Communicating with a waiter or waitress • Adjectives to describe the healthfulness of food	• <u>There is</u> and <u>there are</u> with count and non-count nouns • <u>Anything</u> and <u>nothing</u>: common errors • Definite article <u>the</u>: usage **GRAMMAR BOOSTER** • Non-count nouns: usage, expressing quantities • <u>How much</u> / <u>How many</u> • Count nouns: Spelling rules • <u>Some</u> and <u>any</u>

5 **Technology and You** page 50	• Suggest a brand or model
	• Express frustration and sympathy
	• Describe features of products
	• Complain when things don't work
		• Electronic products
		• Household appliances and machines
		• Features of manufactured products
		• Ways to state a problem
		• Ways to sympathize
		• Positive and negative adjectives
			• The present continuous (review):
			  ○ Actions in progress and future plans
			  ○ Statements and questions
			
			GRAMMAR BOOSTER
			• The present continuous: form and spelling rules

Conversation Strategies	Listening/ Pronunciation	Reading	Writing
• Begin responses with a question to confirm • Use Let's to suggest a course of action • Ask personal questions to indicate friendliness • Intensify an informal answer with sure	**Listening Skills:** • Listen for details • Infer information **Pronunciation:** • Intonation of questions	**Texts:** • An enrollment form • Personal profiles • A photo story **Skills/strategies:** • Infer information • Scan for facts	**Task:** • Write a description of a classmate **WRITING BOOSTER** • Capitalization
• Use Really? to express enthusiasm • Provide reasons to decline an invitation • Use Too bad to express disappointment • Repeat with rising intonation to confirm information • Use Thanks, anyway to acknowledge an unsuccessful attempt to help	**Listening Skills:** • Infer a speaker's intention • Listen for main ideas • Listen for details • Listen for locations **Pronunciation:** • Rising intonation to confirm information	**Texts:** • A music website • An entertainment events page • Authentic interviews • A survey of musical tastes • A photo story **Skills/strategies:** • Interpret maps and diagrams • Identify supporting details • Make personal comparisons	**Task:** • Write a short personal essay about one's musical tastes **WRITING BOOSTER** • The sentence
• Use Actually to introduce a topic • Respond to good news with Congratulations! • Respond to bad news with I'm sorry to hear that • Use Thanks for asking to acknowledge an inquiry of concern • Use Well to introduce a lengthy reply • Ask follow-up questions to keep a conversation going	**Listening Skills:** • Infer information • Understand key details • Identify similarities and differences • Listen to take notes • Listen for main ideas • Listen for details **Pronunciation:** • Blending sounds	**Texts:** • Family tree diagrams • A self-help website • A cultural-information survey • A photo story **Skills/strategies:** • Interpret a diagram • Confirm facts • Infer information	**Task:** • Make a Venn diagram • Compare two people in a family **WRITING BOOSTER** • Combining sentences with and or but
• Use Could you …? to make a polite request • Use Sure to agree to a request • Clarify a request by asking for more specific information • Indicate a sudden thought with Actually • Use I'll have to order from a server • Increase politeness with please	**Listening Skills:** • Listen to take notes • Infer the location of a conversation • Listen to predict **Pronunciation:** • The before consonant and vowel sounds	**Texts:** • Menus • A nutrition website • A photo story **Skills/strategies:** • Interpret a map • Understand from context • Infer information	**Task:** • Write a short article about food for a travel newsletter **WRITING BOOSTER** • Connecting words and ideas: and, in addition
• Use Hey or How's it going for an informal greeting • Use What about…? to offer a suggestion • Use Really? to indicate surprise • Use You know to introduce a topic • Express sympathy when someone is frustrated	**Listening Skills:** • Listen to predict • Infer meaning • Listen for details **Pronunciation:** • Intonation of questions	**Texts:** • Newspaper advertisements • A magazine ad for a new product • A photo story **Skills/strategies:** • Understand from context • Activate language from a text	**Task:** • Write a paragraph describing a product **WRITING BOOSTER** • Placement of adjectives

Unit	Communication Goals	Vocabulary	Grammar
6 **Staying in Shape** page 62	• Plan an activity with someone • Talk about habitual activities • Discuss fitness and eating habits • Describe someone's routines	• Physical activities • Places for physical activities • Frequency adverbs: expansion	• <u>Can</u> and <u>have to</u>: meaning, form, and usage • The present continuous and the simple present tense (review) • The present continuous: common errors **GRAMMAR BOOSTER** • Non-action verbs • Frequency adverbs: common errors • Time expressions • More on <u>can</u> and <u>have to</u>
7 **On Vacation** page 74	• Greet someone arriving from a trip • Ask about someone's vacation • Discuss vacation preferences • Describe good and bad travel experiences	• Adjectives to describe trips and vacations • Intensifiers • Ways to describe good and bad travel experiences	• The past tense of <u>be</u> (review): statements and questions • The simple past tense (review): statements and questions • Regular and irregular verb forms **GRAMMAR BOOSTER** • The past tense of <u>be</u>: explanation of form • The simple past tense: more on spelling, usage, and form
8 **Shopping for Clothes** page 86	• Shop and pay for clothes • Ask for a different size or color • Navigate a mall or department store • Discuss clothing do's and don'ts	• Clothing departments • Types of clothing and shoes • Clothing that comes in "pairs" • Interior store locations and directions • Formality and appropriateness in clothing	• Uses of object pronouns • Object pronouns: common errors • Comparative adjectives **GRAMMAR BOOSTER** • Direct and indirect objects: usage rules • Spelling rules for comparative adjectives
9 **Taking Transportation** page 98	• Discuss schedules and buy tickets • Book travel services • Understand airport announcements • Describe transportation problems	• Kinds of tickets and trips • Travel services • Airline passenger information • Flight problems • Transportation problems • Means of public transportation	• Modals <u>should</u> and <u>could</u>: statements and questions • <u>Be going to</u> to express the future: review and expansion **GRAMMAR BOOSTER** • Modals: form, meaning, common errors • Expansion: future actions
10 **Shopping Smart** page 110	• Ask for a recommendation • Bargain for a lower price • Discuss showing appreciation for service • Describe where to get the best deals	• Financial terms • How to bargain • How to describe good and bad deals	• Superlative adjectives • <u>Too</u> and <u>enough</u>: usage and common errors **GRAMMAR BOOSTER** • Superlative adjectives: usage and form • Comparatives (review) • Usage: <u>very</u>, <u>really</u>, and <u>too</u>

Conversation Strategies	Listening/ Pronunciation	Reading	Writing

Conversation Strategies	Listening/ Pronunciation	Reading	Writing
• Use <u>Why don't we . . . ?</u> to suggest an activity • Say <u>Sorry, I can't</u> to apologize for turning down an invitation • Provide a reason with <u>have to</u> to decline an invitation • Use <u>Well, how about . . . ?</u> to suggest an alternative • Use <u>How come?</u> to ask for a reason • Use a negative question to confirm information	**Listening Skills:** • Infer meaning • Infer information • Listen for main ideas • Listen for details • Apply and personalize information **Pronunciation:** • <u>Can</u> / <u>can't</u> • The third-person singular <u>-s</u>	**Texts:** • A bar graph • A fitness survey • A magazine article • A photo story **Skills/strategies:** • Interpret a bar graph • Infer information • Summarize	**Task:** • Write an interview about health and exercise habits **WRITING BOOSTER** • Punctuation of statements and questions
• Say <u>Welcome back!</u> to indicate enthusiasm about someone's return from a trip • Acknowledge someone's interest with <u>Actually</u> • Decline an offer of assistance with <u>That's OK. I'm fine.</u> • Confirm that an offer is declined with <u>Are you sure?</u> • Use <u>Absolutely</u> to confirm a response • Show enthusiasm with <u>No kidding!</u> and <u>Tell me more</u>	**Listening Skills:** • Listen for main ideas • Listen for details • Infer meaning **Pronunciation:** • The simple past tense ending: regular verbs	**Texts:** • Travel brochures • Personal travel stories • A vacation survey • A photo story **Skills/strategies:** • Activate language from a text • Draw conclusions • Identify supporting details	**Task:** • Write a guided essay about a vacation **WRITING BOOSTER** • Time order
• Use <u>Excuse me</u> to indicate you didn't understand or couldn't hear • Use <u>Excuse me</u> to begin a conversation with a clerk • Follow a question with more information for clarification • Acknowledge someone's assistance with <u>Thanks for your help</u> • Respond to gratitude with <u>My pleasure</u>	**Listening Skills:** • Infer the appropriate location • Infer the locations of conversations • Understand locations and directions **Pronunciation:** • Contrastive stress for clarification	**Texts:** • A clothing catalogue • Simple and complex diagrams and plans • A travel blog • A personal opinion survey • A photo story **Skills/strategies:** • Paraphrase • Identify supporting details • Apply information	**Task:** • Write an e-mail or letter explaining what clothes to pack **WRITING BOOSTER** • Connecting ideas with <u>because</u> and <u>since</u>
• Use <u>I'm sorry</u> to respond with disappointing information • Use <u>Well</u> to introduce an alternative. • Use <u>I hope so</u> to politely respond to an offer of help • Use <u>Let me check</u> to buy time to get information	**Listening Skills:** • Infer the type of travel service • Understand public announcements • Listen for details • Use reasoning to evaluate statements of fact **Pronunciation:** • Intonation for stating alternatives	**Texts:** • Transportation schedules • Public transportation tickets • Arrival and departure boards • Newspaper articles • A photo story **Skills/strategies:** • Make decisions based on schedules and needs • Critical thinking	**Task:** • Write two paragraphs about trips **WRITING BOOSTER** • The paragraph
• Use <u>Well</u> to connect an answer to an earlier question • Use <u>How about . . .?</u> to make a financial offer • Use <u>OK</u> to indicate that an agreement has been reached	**Listening Skills:** • Listen for details • Listen for main ideas **Pronunciation:** • Rising intonation for clarification	**Texts:** • A travel guide • A magazine article • Personal travel stories • A photo story **Skills/strategies:** • Draw conclusions • Apply information	**Task:** • Write a guide to your city, including information on where to stay, visit, and shop **WRITING BOOSTER** • Connecting contradictory ideas: <u>even though</u>, <u>however</u>, <u>on the other hand</u>

To the Teacher

What is *Top Notch*?

Top Notch is a six-level* communicative course that prepares adults and young adults to interact successfully and confidently with both native and non-native speakers of English.

The goal of the *Top Notch* course is to make English unforgettable through:

► Multiple exposures to new language
► Numerous opportunities to practice it
► Deliberate and intensive recycling

The *Top Notch* course has two beginning levels: *Top Notch* Fundamentals for true beginners and *Top Notch* 1 for false beginners.

Each full level of *Top Notch* contains enough material for 60 to 90 hours of classroom instruction. A wide choice of supplementary components makes it easy to tailor *Top Notch* to the needs of your classes.

*Summit 1 and *Summit* 2 are the titles of the fifth and sixth levels of the *Top Notch* course. All Student's Books are available in split editions with bound-in workbooks.

The *Top Notch* instructional design

Daily confirmation of progress

Each easy-to-follow two-page lesson begins with a clearly stated communication goal. All lesson activities are integrated with the goal and systematically build toward a final speaking activity in which students demonstrate achievement of the goal. "Can-do" statements in each unit ensure students' awareness of the continuum of their progress.

A purposeful conversation syllabus

Memorable conversation models provide essential and practical social language that students can carry "in their pockets" for use in real life. Guided conversation pair work enables students to modify, personalize, and extend each model so they can use it to communicate their <u>own</u> thoughts and needs. Free discussion activities are carefully crafted so students can continually retrieve and use the language from the models. All conversation models are informed by the Longman Corpus of Spoken American English.

An emphasis on cultural fluency

Recognizing that English is a global language, *Top Notch* actively equips students to interact socially with people from a variety of cultures and deliberately prepares them to understand accented speakers from diverse language backgrounds.

Intensive vocabulary development

Students actively work with a rich vocabulary of high-frequency words, collocations, and expressions in all units of the Student's Book. Clear illustrations and definitions clarify meaning and provide support for independent study, review, and test preparation. Systematic recycling promotes smooth and continued acquisition of vocabulary from the beginning to the advanced levels of the course.

A dynamic approach to grammar

An explicit grammar syllabus is supported by charts containing clear grammar rules, relevant examples, and explanations of meaning and use. Numerous grammar exercises provide focused practice, and grammar usage is continually activated in communication exercises that illustrate the grammar being learned.

A dedicated pronunciation syllabus

Focused pronunciation, rhythm, and intonation practice is included in each unit, providing application of each pronunciation point to the target language of the unit and facilitating comprehensible pronunciation.

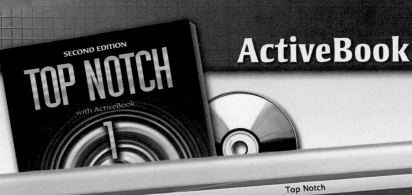

ActiveBook

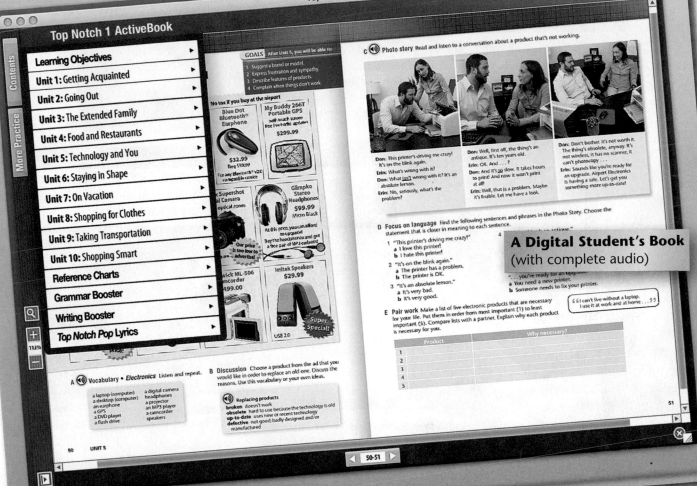

A Digital Student's Book (with complete audio)

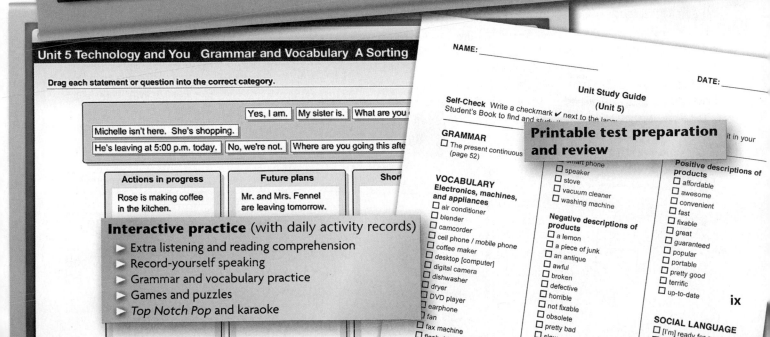

Interactive practice (with daily activity records)
- Extra listening and reading comprehension
- Record-yourself speaking
- Grammar and vocabulary practice
- Games and puzzles
- *Top Notch Pop* and karaoke

Printable test preparation and review

The Teacher's Edition and Lesson Planner

Includes:
- ► A bound-in Methods Handbook for professional development
- ► Detailed lesson plans with suggested teaching times
- ► Language, culture, and corpus notes
- ► Student's Book and Workbook answer keys
- ► Audioscripts
- ► *Top Notch TV* teaching notes

ActiveTeach

- ► A Digital Student's Book with interactive whiteboard (IWB) software
- ► Instantly accessible audio and *Top Notch TV* video
- ► Interactive exercises from the Student's *ActiveBook* for in-class use
- ► A complete menu of printable extension activities

Teacher's Edition and Lesson Planner with ActiveTeach
SECOND EDITION
TOP NOTCH 1
Joan Saslow • Allen Ascher

The Digital Student's Book
With zoom, write, highlight, save and other IWB tools.

Top Notch TV
A hilarious situation comedy, authentic unrehearsed on-the-street interviews, and *Top Notch Pop* karaoke.

Printable Extension Activities
Including:
- • Writing process worksheets
- • Vocabulary flashcards
- • Learning strategies
- • Graphic organizers
- • Pronunciation activities
- • Video activity worksheets and more . . .

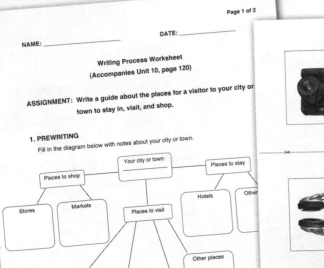

Page 1 of 2

NAME: _____   DATE: _____

Writing Process Worksheet
(Accompanies Unit 10, page 120)

ASSIGNMENT: Write a guide about the places for a visitor to your city or town to stay in, visit, and shop.

1. PREWRITING
Fill in the diagram below with notes about your city or town.

Electronics

Electronics

NAME: _____

Learning Strategy
(Unit 6, page 70, Reading)

READING STRATEGY: skimming

When you read an article, skim for the main ideas first <u>before</u> you read for details.

In the article below, the unimportant parts have been deleted. Notice how much you can understand with fewer words in the article.

When You Think You Can't . . .
Mark Zupan

▭ — accident in 1993 — Mark Zupan - quadriplegic — changed his life — cannot move — arms or legs —

— plays quad rugby — winning a gold medal in — 2008 —. — gives talks — raises money for his sport. — — lifts weights — drives a car, — goes to rock concerts. — careful about — diet —

Bethany Hamilton

▭ — Bethany Hamilton — — in 2003, she lost her — arm — attacked by - shark —. Three weeks later, she – surfing —

Other components

Workbook

Daily assignments that reinforce each lesson.

Classroom Audio Program

Includes a variety of authentic regional and non-native accents.

Complete Assessment Package

Ready-made achievement tests. Software provides option to edit, delete, or add items.

Full-Course Placement Tests

Choose printable or online version.

Copy & Go

Board games, role plays, information gaps, and "find someone who. . ." for every lesson.

MyTopNotchLab

An optional online learning tool with:

- ► An interactive *Top Notch* Workbook
- ► Speaking and writing activities
- ► Pop-up grammar help
- ► Student's Book *Grammar Booster* exercises
- ► *Top Notch TV* with extensive viewing activities
- ► Automatically-graded achievement tests
- ► Easy course management and record-keeping

Getting Acquainted

Why are you studying English?

☐ to travel

☐ to study

☐ to do business

Did You Know?
In 2016, there will be 2 billion English speakers around the world. –from **English Next** (British Council)

☐ to get to know people who don't speak my language

☐ other:

Please complete the form.

Title: ☐ Mr. ☐ Mrs. ☐ Ms. ☐ Miss

Last/Family Name

First/Given Name

Nationality

Occupation

A Pair work Why are you studying English? Compare reasons with a partner.

B Class survey How many students in your class are studying English . . .

.... to do business?   .... to study?   .... (other reasons)
.... to get to know people?   .... to travel?

C 🔊 **Photo story** Read and listen to people getting to know each other.

1:02

Susan: I'll bet this is your dad.

Cara: Yes, it is. Dad, I'd like to introduce you to my friend, Susan Grant.

Sam: It's a pleasure to meet you, Susan. Samuel Pike.

Susan: Great to meet you, too. But please, everyone calls me by my nickname, Suzy.

Sam: And just call me Sam. So, what do you do, Suzy?

Susan: I'm a photographer . . . Oh, I'm sorry. There's my husband . . . Ted, over here!

Ted: Sorry I'm late.

Susan: Ted, this is Cara's dad.

Ted: Oh, how nice to meet you, Mr. Pike!

Sam: Likewise. But please call me Sam.

D Focus on language Look at the underlined expressions in the Photo Story. With a partner, find:

1 two expressions you can use when you introduce people.

2 three expressions you can use when you meet someone.

3 three expressions you can use when you don't want to be formal.

🔊 **Formal titles**

Men	Women
Mr.	Ms. (married or single)
	Mrs. (married)
	Miss (single)

Use titles with family names, not given names.

Ms. Grant NOT ~~Ms. Suzy~~

1:03

E Complete your response to each person.

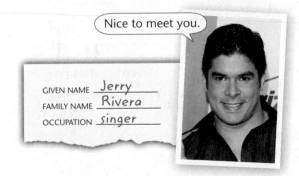

Nice to meet you.

GIVEN NAME *Jerry*
FAMILY NAME *Rivera*
OCCUPATION *singer*

Good to meet you.

GIVEN NAME *Naomi*
FAMILY NAME *Watts*
OCCUPATION *actress*

1 Nice to meet you, too, ...
   a Mr. Jerry
   b Mr. Rivera
   c Ms. Rivera

2 Good to meet you, too, ...
   a Ms. Watts
   b Ms. Naomi
   c Mr. Watts

F Role play Imagine your partner is a famous person. Introduce your partner to the class. Use formal titles.

> ❝I'd like you to meet Jerry Rivera. Mr. Rivera is a singer. ❞

GOAL   Meet someone new

CONVERSATION MODEL

A 🔊)) 1:04 Read and listen to people meeting someone new.

A: Who's that?

B: Over there? I think she's new.

A: Well, let's say hello.

. . .

B: Good morning. I'm Alex, and this is Lauren.

C: Hi. My name's Kathryn Gao. But everyone calls me Kate.

A: Great to meet you, Kate. Where are you from?

C: New York.

B 🔊)) 1:05 **Rhythm and intonation** Listen again and repeat. Then practice the Conversation Model with two partners.

GRAMMAR   *Information questions with be: Review*

| Who's your teacher? | She's Ms. Nieto. |
| Who are they? | They're my classmates. |

| Where's she from? | She's from Argentina. |
| What city are you from? | We're from Los Angeles. |

| What's his e-mail address? | It's ted@kr.com [say "ted at k-r-dot-com"] |
| What are their names? | Andrea and Steven. |

| How old is your brother? | He's twenty-six. |
| How old are they? | She's twelve, and her little sister is eight. |

Contractions
Who's = Who is	**I'm** = I am	**you're** = you are
Where's = Where is	**he's** = he is	**we're** = we are
What's = What is	**she's** = she is	**they're** = they are
	it's = it is	

GRAMMAR BOOSTER ▸ p. 123

- *Information questions with be: usage and form*
- *Possessive nouns and adjectives (review)*

A Grammar practice Complete the conversations. Use contractions of the verb *be* when possible.

1 A: .... that over there?

   B: Oh, that's Hasna. .... from Lebanon.

   A: .... she? She looks very young.

   B: I think .... twenty-five.

2 A: Your new neighbor seems nice.
   .... his name?

   B: His .... Ricardo.

   A: .... he from?

   B: Guatemala.

3 A: .... they?

B: I think .... new students.

A: .... their names?

B: Mieko and Rika.

4 A: It was nice to meet your brothers.
.... they?

B: Greg's only fourteen. But my older brother, David, is twenty-eight.

A: .... David's occupation?

B: .... a lawyer.

5 A: I'll call you sometime. .... your phone number?

B: .... 555-0296. .... yours?

A: 555-8747.

6 A: .... your e-mail address? I'll send you a note.

B: .... choi23@kr.com.

A: K - r - dot - com? That's interesting. .... you from?

B: Pusan, Korea. I'm here on business.

B Grammar practice Write at least four information questions for your partner.

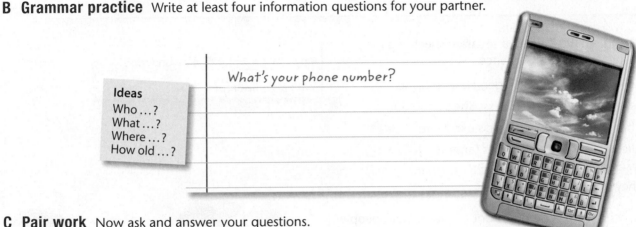

Ideas
Who ...?
What ...?
Where ...?
How old ...?

What's your phone number?

C Pair work Now ask and answer your questions.

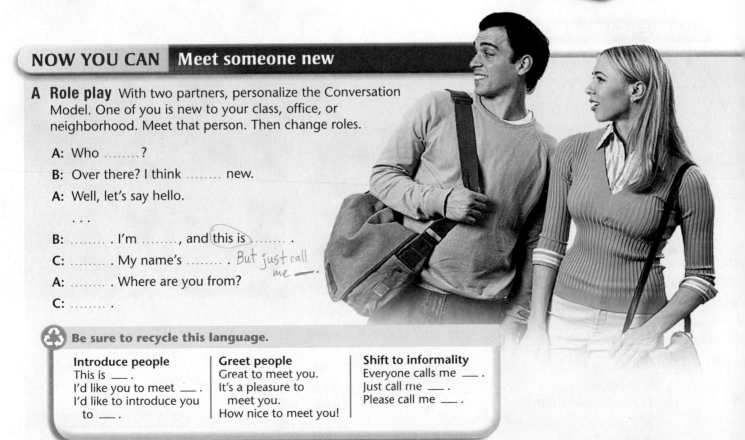

NOW YOU CAN   Meet someone new

A Role play With two partners, personalize the Conversation Model. One of you is new to your class, office, or neighborhood. Meet that person. Then change roles.

A: Who ....?

B: Over there? I think .... new.

A: Well, let's say hello.

. . .

B: .... I'm ...., and this is ....

C: .... My name's .... But just call me ——.

A: .... Where are you from?

C: ....

♻ **Be sure to recycle this language.**

Introduce people	Greet people	Shift to informality
This is ——.	Great to meet you.	Everyone calls me ——.
I'd like you to meet ——.	It's a pleasure to meet you.	Just call me ——.
I'd like to introduce you to ——.	How nice to meet you!	Please call me ——.

B Change partners Practice the conversation again. Meet other people.

GOAL Identify and describe people

GRAMMAR *Modification with adjectives: Review*

Adjectives describe nouns and pronouns. They can go after the verb <u>be</u> or before a noun.
Alejandro Sanz is **handsome**. He's a **handsome singer** from Spain.
Tony Leung and Gong Li are **famous**. They're **famous actors** from China.

Use an article before an adjective that modifies a singular noun.
He's **a** great musician.   NOT ~~He's great musician~~.

> **Positive adjectives**
> beautiful
> great
> excellent
> famous
> handsome
> wonderful
> fantastic
> terrific

A Grammar practice On a separate sheet of paper, combine each pair of sentences.

> Amy Tan is a writer. She's wonderful.
>
> *She's a wonderful writer.*

1 Juan Luis Guerra is a singer. He's fantastic.

2 Penélope Cruz is an actress. She's beautiful.

3 Zhong Biao is an artist. He's excellent.

4 Alice Waters is a chef. She's famous.

5 Eric Clapton and Jeff Beck are musicians. They're great.

B Now write three sentences about other famous people.

CONVERSATION MODEL

A 🔊 1:06 Read and listen to someone identify and describe a person.

A: Hey. Who's John Mayer?

B: You don't know? For real?

A: No. Is he famous?

B: He sure is. He's a great musician.

A: Where's he from?

B: The United States.

B 🔊 1:07 **Rhythm and intonation** Listen again and repeat. Then practice the Conversation Model with a partner.

JOHN MAYER

GRAMMAR <u>Yes</u> / <u>no</u> questions and short answers with <u>be</u>: Review

Are you our teacher?	Yes, I **am**.	No, I'm **not**.
Is she Chinese?	Yes, she **is**.	No, she **isn't**. [No, she's **not**.]
Is your nickname Josh?	Yes, it **is**.	No, it **isn't**. [No, it's **not**.]
Are you and Tom students?	Yes, we **are**.	No, we **aren't**. [No, we're **not**.]
Are they famous?	Yes, they **are**.	No, they **aren't**. [No, they're **not**.]

> **Be careful!**
> Yes, I am. NOT ~~Yes, I'm.~~
> Yes, she is. NOT ~~Yes, she's.~~

> **GRAMMAR BOOSTER** ▸ p. 124
> • <u>Yes</u> / <u>no</u> questions: usage and form
> • Common errors

A Find the grammar Find two information questions and one <u>yes</u> / <u>no</u> question with <u>be</u> in the Conversation Model on page 6.

B Grammar practice Complete the questions and answers. Use contractions when possible.

1 A: .... your father a teacher?
   B: Yes, ...

2 A: .... your son an athlete?
   B: No, ...an
      artist.

3 A: .... this your new address?
   B: Yes, ...

4 A: Who .... those new students?
      .... from Canada?
   B: No, ... I think .... from
      the U.K.

5 A: That's a nice hat! .... new?
   B: No, ...

6 A: .... you a musician?
   B: Yes, ... a violinist.

PRONUNCIATION   *Intonation of questions*

1:08
A ◀)) Use rising intonation in yes / no questions. Use falling intonation in information questions. Read and listen. Then listen again and repeat.

1 Is this his e-mail address?

2 Are they from Canada?

3 What's his e-mail address?

4 Where are they from?

B Pair work Write three <u>yes</u> / <u>no</u> questions and three information questions with <u>be</u>. Then take turns practicing question intonation.

NOW YOU CAN   Identify and describe people

A Look at the famous people. Add information about a famous person you know.

B Pair work Use the information about the people. Change the Conversation Model to practice asking for and providing information about each person. Use your own adjective. Then change roles.

A: Hey. Who's ....?
B: You don't know? For real?
A: No. Is .... famous?
B: .... sure is.
A: Where .... from?
B: ....

C Change partners Practice the conversation again. Talk about other famous people.

Javier Bardem
actor (Spain)

Diana Krall
musician (Canada)

Patricia Yeo
chef (U.S.)

Your own famous person
first name ....
last name ....
occupation ....
country ....
adjective to describe the person
....

GOAL **Provide personal information**

BEFORE YOU LISTEN

A 🔊 1:09 **Vocabulary • *Personal information*** Read and listen. Then listen again and repeat.

nationality He is originally from India, but his nationality is Canadian. He has a Canadian passport.

birthplace I'm from Mexico City, but it isn't my birthplace. I was born in a beautiful small town called Patzcuaro.

hometown She was born in Seoul, but her hometown is Pusan. She grew up there.

B **Pair work** Ask your partner questions, using the Vocabulary.

❝ What's your birthplace? ❞

1:10
🔊 **Countries and nationalities**

Country	Nationality
I'm from **Japan**.	I'm **Japanese**.
She's from **China**.	She's **Chinese**.
She's from **Canada**.	She's **Canadian**.
They're from **Argentina**.	They're **Argentinean**.
He's from the **U.K.**	He's **British**.
We're from **Turkey**.	We're **Turkish**.

See page 122 for a more complete list.

LISTENING COMPREHENSION

A 🔊 1:11 **Listen for details** Listen to each conversation and write each person's nationality and occupation. Then check <u>yes</u> or <u>no</u> to indicate whether the person has a nickname.

	Nationality	Occupation	Nickname?
1	_____	_____	☐ yes ☐ no
2	_____	_____	☐ yes ☐ no
3	_____	_____	☐ yes ☐ no
4	_____	_____	☐ yes ☐ no

a computer programmer

an interpreter

a graphic designer

a salesperson

B 🔊 1:12 **Infer information** Now listen to each conversation again and complete each statement.

1 He grew up in ....
  a Ankara   **b** London   **c** Izmir

2 Her birthplace is ....
  a Osaka   **b** Tokyo   **c** Seoul

3 She's originally from ....
  a Buenos Aires   **b** Montevideo   **c** Santiago

4 His hometown is ....
  a Chicago   **b** Toronto   **c** New York

Partner A: Look at the top of the page.
Partner B: Turn your book and look at the bottom of the page.
Ask information questions with <u>be</u> and write the missing personal information.

If you don't understand, ask:
Could you repeat that?
How do you spell that?

PARTNER A

Name: Richard Anderson
Nickname: Rick
Occupation: ....
Nationality: British
Birthplace: ....
Age: ....
E-mail: randy@umail.com.uk

Name: Lucia Alberti
Occupation: ....
Age: 26
Nationality: ....
Hometown: ....
E-mail: alberti.lucia@inet.com.it

Name: ....
Occupation: manager
Age: ....
Nationality: Japanese
Hometown: Kyoto
E-mail: ....

Name: ....
Nickname: ....
Occupation: graphic designer
Nationality: ....
Age: 31
Hometown: ....
E-mail: fp52@vmail.com.ve

Name: Lucia Alberti
Occupation: writer
Age: 26
Nationality: Italian
Hometown: Rome
E-mail: alberti.lucia@inet.com.it

Name: Richard Anderson
Nickname: Rick
Occupation: photographer
Nationality: British
Birthplace: Liverpool
Age: 24
E-mail: randy@umail.com.uk

Name: Francisco Pastor
Nickname: Paco
Occupation: graphic designer
Nationality: Venezuelan
Age: 31
Hometown: Maracaibo
E-mail: fp52@vmail.com.ve

Name: Riko Ohira
Occupation: manager
Age: 42
Nationality: Japanese
Hometown: Kyoto
E-mail: rohira@unet.com.jp

If you don't understand, ask:
Could you repeat that?
How do you spell that?

PARTNER B

his occupation
her
you

GOAL   Introduce someone to a group

BEFORE YOU READ

A Warm-up In your life, where do you see or hear English?

B Preview Before you read, search for the word <u>English</u> in the article. Then answer this question: How does each person use English?

READING 1:13

Who Uses English?

MEET LETICIA MARQUES. She works as a financial manager for a Swedish automotive company in Curitiba, Brazil, where she was born and raised. She is single and lives with her parents. "I use English every day," Ms. Marques says. "We use it in most of our e-mails and meetings and for calls to Sweden, the U.S., and France." In her free time, she likes to watch DVDs in English. "It's good for my pronunciation," she says.

THIS IS YUAN YONG JING, his wife, Zheng Yang, and their son, Yuan Bao. They live in Beijing, China. Mr. Yuan, a manager, is originally from Weihai, a small seaside city in Shandong Province. His wife is a teacher, and their son is a middle-school student. "Our company provides tour guides to foreign businesspeople who visit China, so English is very important for my work," he says. At home, Mr. Yuan enjoys watching English-language TV and listening to English-language radio.

MEET MARCUS STOLZE, an information technology researcher. Mr. Stolze lives with his wife, Thérèse, and children, Lena and Jan, in Rüti, a small town in Switzerland. Mr. Stolze is originally from Brilon, Germany. Thérèse is an English teacher and speaks four languages. Their children are also multilingual. "At work, we use English a lot because we communicate with people who speak many different languages," he says. "Also, most good books on computing are in English," he adds.

Source: Authentic interviews of real people

A Infer information Complete each statement.

1 ...... are in English at Ms. Marques's company in Brazil.
   a E-mails
   b Meetings
   c Phone calls
   d E-mails, meetings, and calls

2 In his work, Mr. Yuan uses English ....
   a to teach classes
   b to help businesspeople
   c to watch TV
   d to listen to the radio

3 Mr. Stolze probably uses English with people from ....
   a the United States
   b Switzerland
   c the United Kingdom
   d all over the world

B Scan for facts Complete the information about the people.

	Ms. Marques	Mr. Yuan	Mr. Stolze
Occupation			
Lives in . . .			
Hometown			
Married?	☐ yes ☐ no	☐ yes ☐ no	☐ yes ☐ no

On your *ActiveBook* Self-Study Disc:
Extra Reading Comprehension Questions

NOW YOU CAN   **Introduce someone to a group**

A Read the information about each person. Then complete the two paragraphs below.

Name: Evelyne Hsu
Nickname: Effie
Occupation: office assistant
Hometown: Chia-yi, Taiwan
Birthplace: same
Age: 27
Favorite actor: Tony Leung
Favorite sport: swimming
Other: lives in Kaohsiung

Name: José Antonio Méndez
Nickname: Tonio
Occupation: market researcher
Hometown: Celanova, a small town in Spain
Birthplace: Equatorial Guinea (in Africa)
Age: 48
Other: lives in New York, has two children

This is ...., but everyone calls her .... She's .... years old and she's an .... Ms. .... lives in ...., but she is originally from a city called .... Her favorite actor is ...., and her favorite sport is ....

Meet .... He's a ...., and he lives in .... Everyone calls him .... He's originally from ...., but actually he was born in .... Mr. Méndez is .... years old, and he has ....

B Notepadding Interview a classmate. Write his or her personal information on the notepad.

Name:
Nickname:
Occupation:
Hometown:
Birthplace:
Age:
Favorite actor:
Favorite sport:
Other:

C Group work Introduce your partner to your classmates.

♲ **Be sure to recycle this language.**

This is ___ .
I'd like you to meet ___ .
I'd like to introduce you to ___ .
Everyone calls her / him ___ .
His / her nickname is ___ .
___ is originally from ___ .
His / her hometown is ___ .
His / her favorite ___ is ___ .

11

Review

More Practice

ActiveBook *Self-Study Disc*

grammar · vocabulary · listening
reading · speaking · pronunciation

A ◀)) **Listening comprehension** Listen to the conversations. Then listen
again and write each person's occupation and nationality.

	Name	Occupation	Nationality
1	George Detcheverry		
2	Sonia Pereira		
3	Mark Zaleski		
4	Marjorie Baxter		

Polish   Brazilian
French   Australian

B Complete each statement.

1 We're from (China / Chinese).

2 He's (Australia / Australian).

3 She's from (Italy / Italian).

4 My friend is (Uruguay / Uruguayan).

5 We're from (Japan / Japanese).

6 They're (Chile / Chilean).

7 My neighbors are from (Korea / Korean).

8 We're (Mexico / Mexican).

C Complete each conversation in your own way. (You don't need to give real information.)

1 "What city are you from?"
   YOU ....

2 "What's your e-mail address?"
   YOU ....

3 "Are you a teacher?"
   YOU ....

4 YOU .... ?
   "I'm from Canada."

5 YOU .... ?
   "I'm a graphic designer."

6 YOU ....
   "Great to meet you, too."

D Writing On a separate sheet of paper, write a short description of the classmate you
interviewed on page 11. Include the following information.

• first and last name
• age
• occupation
• hometown
• birthplace

1:15/1:16
♪ **Top Notch Pop**
"It's Nice to Meet You"
Lyrics p. 149

My partner's first name is Peter. His
last name is Hughes. He is twenty...

WRITING BOOSTER ▸ p. 142

• *Capitalization*
• *Guidance for Exercise D*

Pair work

1 Create a conversation for the people in Picture 1. Start like this:

Who's Ricky Martin?

2 With a partner, invent personal information for the people in Picture 2. Then create a conversation for them.

Contest Form teams. Create questions for another team about the web page, using the verb <u>be</u>. (A team gets one point for each correct question and one point for each correct answer.) For example:

What's his nickname?

Celebrity Screens
Web page of the rich and famous

the news   who's who and what's what   the rich and famous ›   forum   guestbook
the rich and famous/ricky martin ›

Ricky Martin: the facts!

Biography

real name: Enrique Martín Morales
occupation: singer and actor
marital status: single
birth date: December 4, 1971
birthplace: San Juan, Puerto Rico

Other information

favorite food: Cuban and Italian
favorite actor: Robert De Niro

NOW I CAN...

☐ Meet someone new.
☐ Identify and describe people.
☐ Provide personal information.
☐ Introduce someone to a group.

Going Out

GOALS   After Unit 2, you will be able to:
1 Accept or decline an invitation.
2 Express locations and give directions.
3 Make plans to see an event.
4 Talk about musical tastes.

My Tunes STORE

GENRES
Rhythm & Blues
Reggae
Rock
Salsa
Classical Music
Folk Music
Movie Soundtracks
Jazz
Show Tunes

FREE DOWNLOADS
Albums
Singles

FEATURES
f Add to Facebook
mp3 Buy MP3s

QUICK LINKS

Browse
Search
Redeem
Support
My Alerts
My Account

THIS WEEK'S SPECIALS   ● ○ ○ ○   See All ➔

Rhythm & Blues

Reggae

Rock

Salsa

Classical Music

Folk Music

Movie Soundtracks

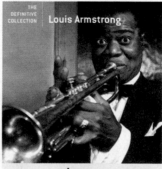
Jazz

Show Tunes

A Look at the online music store site. Do you download music from the Internet? Why or why not?

B 🔊» **Vocabulary • Genres** Listen and repeat.
1:17

C Pair work Tell your partner what you would click on first. Explain why.

D Discussion Which is better—buying a CD in a store or downloading music from the Internet? Explain your answer.

E ◀))) **Photo story** Read and listen to a conversation about music. ^1:18^

Meg: Hey. What's up?
Sara: Not much. Just downloading some new songs.
Meg: Downloading? That's not for me! Too much trouble. How about some live music tonight?
Sara: Sounds good. Where?

Meg: Klepto's playing at midnight at the Spot. Would you like to go?
Sara: At midnight? Sorry. That's past my bedtime.
Meg: Well, River T's there, too. They're playing at 8:00.
Sara: River T—the R&B group? Now that's more my style. I'm a real R&B fan.

Meg: Perfect! Meet you in front of the club at 7:45?
Sara: See you there!

F Focus on language Choose the underlined word or expression from the Photo Story with the same meaning:

1 That's too late for me.
2 Great!
3 music in a concert

4 What are you doing?
5 I like that better.
6 I don't like that.

G Think and explain Choose an answer. Use a quotation to explain your answer.

1 What's Sara doing?
  a getting music from the Internet
  b buying tickets for a concert on the Internet

  > ❝ Sara says, 'Just downloading some new songs.' ❞

2 What does Meg want to do?
  a download music from the Internet
  b go to a concert

3 Which woman doesn't like to go to sleep late?
  a Sara
  b Meg

4 When and where are they going to meet?
  a at midnight at River T
  b at the club before the show

H What kinds of music do you like? Number the music genres in order, making number 1 your favorite.

.... salsa .... rock .... hip-hop

.... movie soundtracks .... classical .... jazz

.... pop .... reggae .... other ....

I Class survey Compare your choices. Which genres do most classmates like?

> ❝ Who chose rock as their favorite? ❞

an electric guitar

GOAL **Accept or decline an invitation**

CONVERSATION MODEL

A 🔊 1:19 Read and listen to an invitation to a movie.

A: Are you free on Saturday? *Batman* is at the Movie Center.

B: Really? I'd love to go. What time?

A: At noon.

To decline . . .

B: Really? I'd love to go, but I'm busy on Saturday.

A: Too bad. Maybe some other time.

B 🔊 1:20 **Rhythm and intonation** Listen again and repeat.
Then practice the Conversation Model with a partner.

GRAMMAR
Prepositions of time and place; Questions with ___When___, ___What time___, *and* ___Where___: *Review*

Prepositions of time
When's the concert? **What time's** the play? It's . . .

on	in	at
on Saturday	in March	at 8:30
on June 7th	in 2009	at noon
on Monday, May 3rd	in the summer	at midnight
on Tuesday morning	in the morning	
	in ten minutes	

Contractions
When's = When is
What time's = What time is
Where's = Where is

Prepositions of place
Where's the play? It's . . .

on	in	at
on Fifth Avenue	in Mexico	at the Film Forum
on the corner	in Osaka	at work
on the street	in the park	at school
on the left	—in the neighborhood	at the art gallery

GRAMMAR BOOSTER ▶ p. 125
• Prepositions of time and place: usage

Grammar practice Complete the e-mail message with prepositions of time and place.

From:	jjlove@meltdown.net
To:	bonnie@vmail.com
Subject:	Salsa dance concert

Hi, Bonnie: Are you busy [   ] Tuesday evening? There's a salsa dance concert right near your office [   ] the Mellon Exhibit Space. Sounds like something really special with dancers from all over the world. It starts [   ] 8:30. I'll be [   ] work until 6:00, but I could meet you [   ] 6:15 or 6:30 [   ] the corner of Grand and Crane. We could have something to eat before the concert. What do you think? —JJ

A 🔊 Read and listen. Then listen again and repeat.

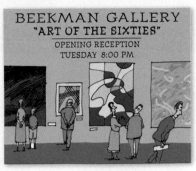

a movie / a film   a play   a concert   a talk / a lecture   an art exhibit

B Pair work Ask and answer questions about the events in the pictures above. Use <u>When</u>, <u>Where</u>, and <u>What time</u>.

❝Where's the talk? ❞

❝It's at Book World. ❞

C 🔊 **Listening comprehension** Listen to the conversations and complete the chart.

	Kind of event	Time of event	Does the person want to go? (Write <u>yes</u>, <u>no</u>, or <u>maybe</u>.)
1			
2			
3			
4			

D 🔊 Listen to the conversations again. Match the event and the place.

.... **1** *Agamemnon*   **a** at the Cinema Center

.... **2** the Boston Symphony Orchestra   **b** at the City Nights Bookstore

.... **3** *Bus Stop*   **c** at the Theater in the Circle

.... **4** Nick Hornby   **d** at the Festival

NOW YOU CAN **Accept or decline an invitation**

A Pair work Change the Conversation Model. Use these events or other events. Decide to accept or decline. Then change roles.

A: Are you free ....? .... is at ....
B: Really? ....

Don't stop!
If you decline, suggest a different event.

♻ **Be sure to recycle this language.**

That's past my bedtime.
That's not for me.
That's more my style.

This Week's Entertainment

MOVIES **Red Sunset**
The Cine Lux, Sat./Sun. 8:55 P.M.

MUSIC **The Soul Brothers**
The Supermarket, Fri. Midnight

TALKS **John Grisham, writer**
Book Town, Mon. 8:00 P.M.

PLAYS **Romeo and Juliet**
The Bridge Theater, Every night 7:30 P.M.

B Change partners Practice the conversation again. Use different events.

GOAL Express locations and give directions

CONVERSATION MODEL

A 🔊 1:24 Read and listen to someone asking for and getting directions.

A: Excuse me. I'm looking for the National Bank.

B: The National Bank? Do you know the address?

A: Yes. It's 205 Holly Avenue.

B: Oh. Walk to the corner of First and Holly. It's right around the corner, across from the museum.

Or if you don't know . . .

B: The National Bank? I'm sorry. I'm not from around here.

A: Thanks, anyway.

B 🔊 1:25 **Rhythm and intonation** Listen again and repeat. Then practice the Conversation Model with a partner.

VOCABULARY *Locations and directions*

A 🔊 1:26 Read and listen. Then listen again and repeat.

Locations Where is the _____ ?

It's **on the right side** of the street.

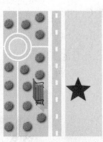

It's **across from** the park.

It's **down the street from** the museum.

It's **around the corner from** the theater.

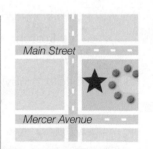

It's **between** Main (Street) **and** Mercer (Avenue).

Directions How do I get to the _____ ?

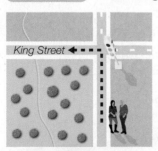

Turn left at the corner / **at** the light / **on** King Street.

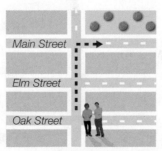

Go / Walk / Drive **two blocks and turn right**.

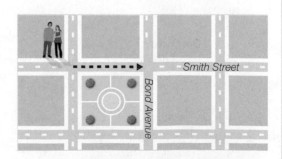

Go / Walk / Drive **to the corner of** Smith (Street) **and** Bond (Avenue).

B 🔊 **Listening comprehension** Listen to the conversations and write the number of each place the people talk about on the map. (Be careful: There are three places but seven boxes.)

1:27

C Pair work Use the vocabulary of location to tell your partner where you live.

> 66 My house is on Grove Street, between Dodd Street and Park Street. 99

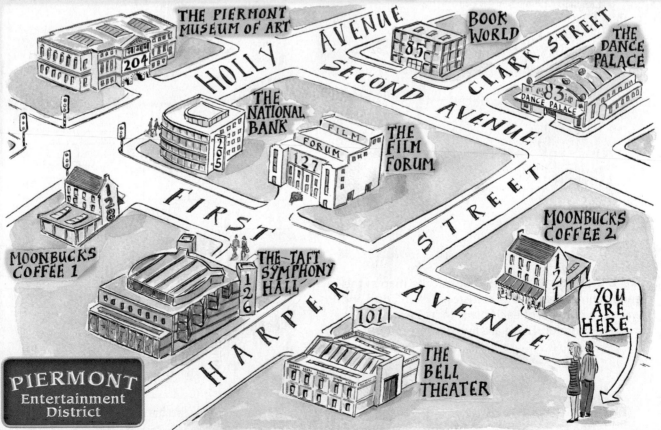

PRONUNCIATION *Rising intonation to confirm information*

A 🔊 Repeat information with rising intonation to be sure you understand. Read and listen. Then listen again and repeat.

1:28

A: Where's the library?
B: The library?

A: Let's meet at the mall.
B: The mall?

B Pair work Talk about two other places to practice confirming information.

NOW YOU CAN   Express locations and give directions

A Pair work Use the Vocabulary and the Piermont map (or a map of your own town or neighborhood) to change the Conversation Model. Then change roles.

A: Excuse me. I'm looking for ....
B: ....? Do you know the address?
A: Yes. It's ....
B: Oh. ....

Don't stop!
Ask about other locations.

B Change partners Ask about other locations and give directions.

GOAL | Make plans to see an event

BEFORE YOU LISTEN

Preview Look at the tickets below. What kinds of events are included in the Kingston Culturefest?

LISTENING COMPREHENSION

A 1:29 **Listen for details** Listen to people calling the Kingston Culturefest. Look at the tickets. Then listen again and complete the information in the boxes.

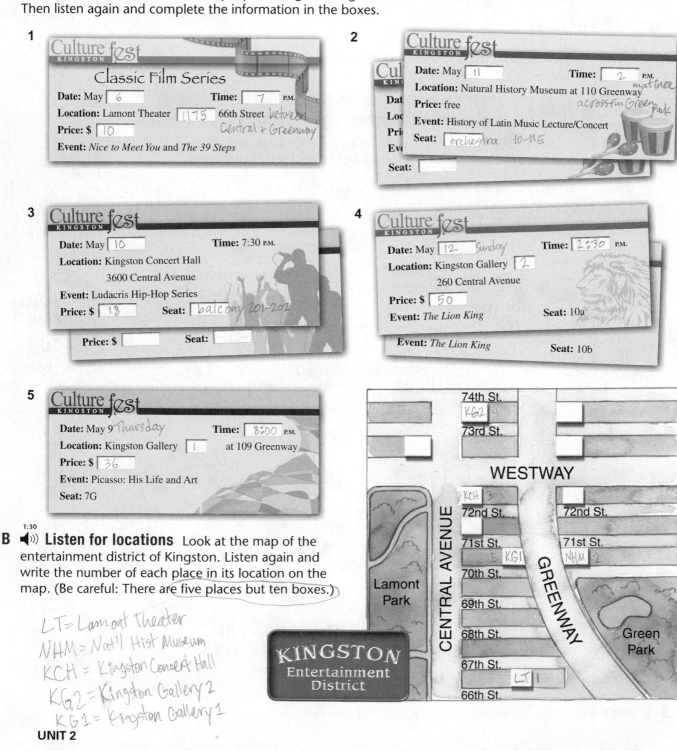

1

Culture fest
KINGSTON

Classic Film Series
Date: May [6]   **Time:** [7] P.M.
Location: Lamont Theater [1175] 66th Street *between Central + Greenway*
Price: $ [10]
Event: *Nice to Meet You* and *The 39 Steps*

2

Culture fest
KINGSTON

Date: May [11]   **Time:** [2] P.M. *matinee*
Location: Natural History Museum at 110 Greenway *across from Green park*
Price: free
Event: History of Latin Music Lecture/Concert
Seat: [orchestra 10-11E]

Seat: [ ]

3

Culture fest
KINGSTON

Date: May [10]   **Time:** 7:30 P.M.
Location: Kingston Concert Hall
   3600 Central Avenue
Event: Ludacris Hip-Hop Series
Price: $ [18]   **Seat:** [balcony 201-202]

Price: $ [ ]   **Seat:** [ ]

4

Culture fest
KINGSTON

Date: May [12] *Sunday*   **Time:** [2:30] P.M.
Location: Kingston Gallery [2]
   260 Central Avenue
Price: $ [50]
Event: *The Lion King*   **Seat:** 10a

Event: *The Lion King*   **Seat:** 10b

5

Culture fest
KINGSTON

Date: May 9 *Thursday*   **Time:** [8:00] P.M.
Location: Kingston Gallery [1]   at 109 Greenway
Price: $ [36]
Event: Picasso: His Life and Art
Seat: 7G

B 1:30 **Listen for locations** Look at the map of the entertainment district of Kingston. Listen again and write the number of each place in its location on the map. (Be careful: There are five places but ten boxes.)

LT = Lamont Theater
NHM = Nat'l Hist Museum
KCH = Kingston Concert Hall
KG2 = Kingston Gallery 2
KG1 = Kingston Gallery 1

Map labels: 74th St. | KG2 [4] | 73rd St. | WESTWAY | KCH [3] | 72nd St. | 72nd St. | 71st St. | [5] KG1 | NHM [2] | 71st St. | 70th St. | Lamont Park | CENTRAL AVENUE | GREENWAY | 69th St. | 68th St. | Green Park | 67th St. | LT [1] | 66th St.

KINGSTON Entertainment District

A Notepadding Read about all the events for the week of May 6–12 below and on the tickets on page 20. Choose events you'd like to see. Write those events, times, and places on the notepad.

Event	Day / Date / Time	Place

Kingston Post

THIS WEEK at the **KINGSTON Culture fest** HIGHLIGHTS

MAY

MON	TUES	WED	THURS	FRI	SAT	SUN
6	**7**	**8**	**9**	**10**	**11**	**12**

THEATER

Neil Simon's classic comedy
Barefoot in the Park
Lamont Theater

Tuesday to Friday 8:00 P.M.
Tkts: Balcony from $65
Orchestra from $85

The Indian Ink Theatre Company
The Dentist's Chair

" *A Serious Play For Serious Theatergoers* "

Kingston Gallery 2
Friday and Saturday 8:00 P.M.

TALKS / LECTURES

Global Warming: How It Changes Our World

Al Gore (former vice president of the U.S. and winner of the Nobel Prize)
Tuesday 6:30 P.M. and 9:00 P.M.
Natural History Museum
Free!

GALLERY TALK
The History of Art
Series of Six Lectures
This week: Greek and Roman art with art exhibit included. Janetta Rebold Benton

Monday and Thursday 7:45 P.M.

Kingston Gallery 2
Members' price: $5.00
General admission: $12.00

CONCERTS

Vanessa-Mae, violinist
Vanessa-Mae will play the Tchaikovsky Violin Concerto in D Major with the New York Philharmonic Orchestra

Also: Johann Sebastian Bach's *Toccata and Fugue in D Minor*
Kingston Concert Hall

Wednesday and Saturday: 8:00 P.M.
Sunday: 2:00 P.M. (matinee)
Tkts: $50 (students $25)

GALLERY JAZZ
Cassandra **Wilson**

Singer, songwriter, producer sings from her new album *Loverly,* featuring "Dust my Broom."
Kingston Gallery 2
Tuesday, Wednesday, and Friday 10:00 P.M.
late show: **12:30 A.M.**   Tkts: $23

B Pair work Compare the events you'd like to see. Make plans to see one or more of the events together. Use the map on page 20.

 Be sure to recycle this language.

Invite
Are you free / busy on ___ ?
There's a [play] at ___ .
Would you like to go?

Ask for information
How about ___?
What time's the ___ ?
Where is it?

Accept and decline
I'd love to go.
See you at ___ .
I'd love to go, but ___ .
Maybe some other time.
That's past my bedtime.
I'm [not really] a ___ fan.
That's not for me.
That's more my style.

Locations / Directions
It's across from the ___ .
It's around the corner from the ___ .
It's on the ___ side of the street.
It's between ___ and ___ .
Turn left at ___ .
Go (Walk / Drive) to ___ .

| GOAL | **Talk about musical tastes** |

A Warm-up In what ways is music important to you?

B Preview Read the question at the beginning of the article and the first sentence in each answer. What do you think "musical tastes" are?

READING 1:31

What are your musical tastes?

▶ My favorite genre is alternative rock. I love live concerts. I once saw Metallica and Foo Fighters live in New York. They were awesome. I also like to listen to music when I travel. I just load my mini MP3 player with lots of songs and carry it with me. At home, I like the music channels on TV. I also enjoy music videos and often search for them on the Internet.

Damir Rudic
Systems administrator, IT, Banja Luka City, Bosnia and Herzegovina

▶ I'm a big music fan. I'm into all kinds of music—pop, R&B, jazz, classical—you name it. When I'm really stressed out, classical music helps me relax. I also like to play "oldies" and sing along really loud! In the past, I collected CDs, but now I just buy songs on the Internet. It's really convenient because you don't have to change CDs! I just download the files onto my MP3 player.

Moon-Jeong Curie Lim
Marketing manager, Seoul, Korea

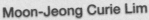

▶ I listen to music on my commute and at home after work. I've got plenty of time to listen because I listen while I do other things, like reading, checking e-mail, or hanging out with friends. I love to see rock bands live, but sometimes I prefer CDs because the sound quality is better. I download music and I pay about one U.S. dollar per song, but even at that price I could never buy all the music I want to listen to!

Adam Klagsbrun
Sales representative, New York, USA

Source: Authentic interviews of real people

A **Identify supporting details** Read the interviews again. Circle T for <u>true</u> or F for <u>false</u> about each statement. Find details in the text to support your answers.

T   F   **1**   Mr. Rudic likes music videos. He says: ....

T   F   **2**   Mr. Rudic only listens to music at home. He says: ....

T   F   **3**   Ms. Lim buys lots of CDs in stores. She says: ....

T   F   **4**   Mr. Klagsbrun always prefers live concerts to CDs. He says: ....

B **Make personal comparisons** Who are you like: Mr. Rudic, Ms. Lim, or Mr. Klagsbrun? Explain how.

> ❝ I'm like Adam Klagsbrun. I listen to music while I do other things. ❞

On your *ActiveBook* Self-Study Disc:
Extra Reading Comprehension Questions

NOW YOU CAN   Talk about musical tastes

A **Frame your ideas** Fill out the survey about your musical tastes.

MUSIC IN YOUR LIFE   TAKE THE SURVEY!

1. Are you a music fan?
  ○ yes   ○ no

2. What's your favorite kind of music?
  ○ rock   ○ pop   ○ classical
  ○ jazz   ○ R&B   ○ rap / hip-hop
  ○ Latin   ○ folk   ○ other ....

3. Who are your favorite artists?
  ....
  ....
  Why? ....
  ....

4. When do you listen to music?
  ○ when I study   ○ when I drive
  ○ when I work   ○ all the time
  ○ other ....

5. Do you go to concerts?
  ○ often   ○ sometimes   ○ never

  If so, what's your favorite kind of concert?
  ....

6. How do you listen to music?
  ○ on CDs   ○ on the Internet
  ○ on the radio   ○ on music videos
  ○ on MP3s   ○ on TV music channels
  ○ on cassettes   ○ other ....

7. How many CDs do you own?
  ○ none   ○ 1–50   ○ 50–100   ○ 100–200
  ○ more than 200

  What kinds of music? ....
  ....

B **Pair work** Compare surveys with a partner. Summarize your answers and your partner's answers on the notepad.

About me	About my partner
I'm a hip-hop fan.	Her favorite music is hip-hop, too.

C **Discussion** Now use the notepad to tell the class about your musical tastes.

> ❝ My partner and I are really into music. We're both hip-hop fans. ❞

Text-mining (optional)
Underline language in the Reading on page 22 to use in the Discussion. For example: "I'm into ____ ."

Review

A 🔊 **Listening comprehension** Listen to the conversations about entertainment and cultural events. Complete the chart with the kind of event and the time of the event.
1:32

B 🔊 Look at the chart and listen again. Circle the event if the person accepts the invitation.
1:33

	Kind of event	Time of event
1		
2		
3		

C Complete each conversation, based on the picture.

1

A: There's a great .... at the City Theater.

B: ....'s the show?

A: Eight o'clock.

2

A: I'm sorry I'm late. This .... is awesome. What time did it start?

B: .... 6:30. Don't worry. You didn't miss much.

3

A: Hello?

B: Hi. I'm calling from the Beekman Gallery. There's an .... of paintings from France.

A: Sounds great! Meet you there .... fifteen minutes?

4

A: Are you free .... Monday evening? Dr. Benson is giving a .... on the native plants of the desert. Do you want to go?

B: That depends. .... time?

A: It's .... 7:00.

D Unscramble the following sentences. Then match the sentences with the pictures. Write the number on the picture.

1 on Martine The bookstore Avenue Street is corner of and the Bank

....

2 8:00 Saturday The exhibit is on August 3 at P.M.

....

3 around the street The movie is the theater corner and down

....

4 corner The house is around the street and across the

....

E **Writing** On a separate sheet of paper, write at least five sentences about yourself and your tastes in music.

My name is Kazu Sato. I'm from Nagoya. I'm a classical music fan. I love Mozart...

WRITING BOOSTER ▸ p. 142
• The sentence
• Guidance for Exercise E

🎵 **Top Notch Pop**
"Going Out"
Lyrics p. 149
1:34/1:35

Contest Form teams. Study the ads for one minute. Then close your books. With your team, name all the events you can remember. (Your team gets one point for each correct event.)

Pair work Create conversations for the two people.

1 Ask and answer questions about the ads.
Use <u>Where</u>, <u>When</u>, and <u>What time</u>. For example:
Q: Where's the lecture?
A: It's . . .

2 Discuss the ads. Make plans, suggestions, and invitations. Discuss your likes and dislikes.

The Journal News- October 22

Today's Entertainment

B16

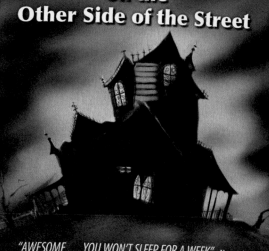

The House
on the
Other Side of the Street

"AWESOME . . . YOU WON'T SLEEP FOR A WEEK" - Newstime
"Don't bring the kids." - Theodore Roper

PLAZA THEATER
237-FILM   10:25 P.M.   1:00 A.M.

MOVIES

In a world where anything could happen, at any time . . .

DO YOU HAVE ANY WATER IN THAT BOTTLE?

"A hilarious spoof of airport culture"
Alizia Compton, *Today's Arts Magazine*

Do You Have Any Liquids?
Mama Cruz   Rachel Weldon

CinePlex 2
5:25, 7:05, 9:30

PLAYS

Wicked
Hill Street Theater
660 North Main
8:30 P.M.

OTHER EVENTS - Talks/Lectures

James M Cowan
A Plan for Everyday Life
Lecture, discussion, book signing
Books and Other Precious Things
400 Jackson Street   6:45 P.M.

MUSIC

Nora Jones
singer / songwriter

TODAY ONLY
City Limits Jazz Club
9:30 P.M.

The China Philharmonic Orchestra with The Shanghai Opera House Chorus
Mozart's Requiem
Symphony Hall, 8:00 P.M.

NOW I CAN...
☐ Accept or decline an invitation.
☐ Express locations and give directions.
☐ Make plans to see an event.
☐ Talk about musical tastes.

25

The Extended Family

GOALS After Unit 3, you will be able to

1 Report news about relationships.
2 Describe extended families.
3 Compare people.
4 Discuss family cultural traditions.

grandparents

my **grandfather**   my **grandmother**

Cliff   Helen

I'm Linda. This is my husband, Tom. And this is my family.

parents

in-laws

my **mother-in-law**   my **father-in-law**

my **uncle**   my **aunt**   my ....   my ....

Jack   Sally

Pete   Pam

Fran   Dan

my **cousins**

Mary   Mark

my **sister-in-law**   my ....   my ....

my **brother-in-law**

Rita   Bill

Jane

Kevin   Kaye

Paul

Evan   Kim

children

my **nephew**   my **niece**

my ....   my ....

A Look at Linda's photo album. Fill in the missing words in the yellow boxes.

B 🔊 **Vocabulary • *The extended family***
Listen and repeat.

2:02

C **Pair work** Ask and answer questions about Linda's relatives. Use <u>Who</u>.

❝ Who's Bill's wife? ❞

❝ Who are Mary and Mark? ❞

❝ Rita. ❞

❝ They're Tom's in-laws. ❞

D 🔊 2:03 **Photo story** Read and listen to two women discussing family photos.

Anna: Who's that guy? Your brother?

Jane: No, that's my brother-in-law, David. He's married to my older sister, Laura. And this is their son, Michael. He's adopted.*

Anna: Do they have any other children?

Jane: Just the one. He's an only child.

Anna: Looks like they're having a great time in New York.

Jane: Actually, they live there.

Anna: They do? Wow! How often do you see them?

Jane: About twice a year.

Anna: And what about these kids?

Jane: They're my younger sister's. Vicky's the girl. And these are her little brothers, Nick and Alex.

Anna: Nick and Alex look so much alike! Are they twins?*

Jane: They are. My sister and her kids all live in Hong Kong.

*adopted: David and Laura aren't Michael's birth parents.

*twins: Nick and Alex were born at the same time.

E **Think and explain** Check <u>true</u>, <u>false</u>, or <u>no info</u>.
Then explain each answer, using information from the Photo Story.

	true	false	no info
1 David is the husband of Anna's older sister.	☐	☐	☐
2 David and Laura have two children.	☐	☐	☐
3 Jane is Laura's younger sister.	☐	☐	☐
4 Jane doesn't have any brothers.	☐	☐	☐
5 Jane has two nieces and one nephew.	☐	☐	☐
6 Vicky, Nick, and Alex are Jane's cousins.	☐	☐	☐

❝ He's Jane's brother-in-law, not Anna's. ❞

F Complete the chart with information about your extended family.
Write the number of people in each category.

I have . . .		
_____ brother(s)	_____ uncle(s)	_____ cousin(s)
_____ sister(s)	_____ aunt(s)	_____ brother(s)-in-law
_____ nephew(s)	_____ niece(s)	_____ sister(s)-in-law

G **Group work** Compare charts with your classmates. Who in your class has a very large extended family?

❝ How many _____s do you have? ❞

GOAL Report news about relationships

VOCABULARY *Relationships and marital status*

A ◀)) 2:04 Read and listen. Then listen again and repeat.

They're **single**.

They're **engaged**.
(He's her **fiancé**. / She's his **fiancée**.)

They're **married**.

They're **separated**.

They're **divorced**.
(He's her **ex-husband**. / She's his **ex-wife**.)

She's **widowed**.

B ◀)) 2:05 **Listening comprehension** Listen to the conversations. Circle the word that completes each statement.

1 The woman is (single / engaged / married).

2 His aunt is (engaged / widowed / divorced).

3 His sister is (engaged / separated / divorced).

4 Her sister is (engaged / separated / divorced).

GRAMMAR *The simple present tense: Review*

Affirmative statements

I **live** in Rio.
I **have** two children.
I **work** in a school.

Claire **lives** in Tokyo.
She **has** one daughter.
She **works** in an office.

Negative statements

I **don't live** in Lima.
I **don't have** any children.

Paul **doesn't live** in Seoul.
He **doesn't have** a son.

Contractions
don't = do not
doesn't = does not

<u>Yes</u> / <u>no</u> **questions and short answers**

Do you **have** any cousins?
Yes, I **do**. / No, I **don't**.

Do they **work** nearby?
Yes, they **do**. / No, they **don't**.

Does she **have** any children?
Yes, she **does**. / No, she **doesn't**.

Does he **work** nearby?
Yes, he **does**. / No, he **doesn't**.

GRAMMAR BOOSTER ▶ p. 126
• The simple present tense:
  usage and form

Grammar practice Complete the questions and answers. Use the simple present tense.

1 (have) A: ...... your cousin .... any children?

B: Yes, she .... She .... two kids—a girl and a boy.

2 (live) A: .... your grandparents .... in Sydney?

B: No, they .... They .... in Ottawa.

3 (work) A: .... your father .... in Quito?

B: Yes, he .... He .... for the government.

4 (like) A: .... your cousin .... hip-hop?

B: No, he .... He .... it at all.

CONVERSATION MODEL

A 🔊 2:06 Read and listen to good news about a relationship.

A: What's new?

B: Actually, I have some good news. My sister just got engaged!

A: That's great. Congratulations!

B: Thanks!

A: So tell me about her fiancé.

B: Well, he works at PBM. He's an engineer.

Or bad news . . .

B: Actually, I have some bad news. My sister just got divorced.

A: I'm sorry to hear that. Is she OK?

B: Yes, she is. Thanks for asking.

B 🔊 2:07 **Rhythm and intonation** Listen again and repeat. Then practice the Conversation Model with a partner.

NOW YOU CAN   Report news about relationships

A Notepadding Imagine that you have good or bad news about someone in your extended family (or use real news). Write notes to plan a conversation.

Relationship to you:
What's the news?
Where does he / she live?
What does he / she do?
Other information:

good news	bad news
got married	got separated
got engaged	got divorced

B Pair work Personalize the Conversation Model to tell your partner your news. Then change roles.

A: What's new?

B: Actually, I have some .... news. My ....

A: ....

Don't stop!
• Ask <u>yes</u> / <u>no</u> questions.
  Is [she] ___? / Does [he] ___? / Do [they] ___ ?
• Use the simple present tense to say more.
  He lives ___.   They have ___.
  She works ___.   They don't have ___.

C Change partners Report other good or bad news.

GOAL **Describe extended families**

VOCABULARY Other family relationships

A 🔊 2:08 Read and listen. Then listen again and repeat.

Barry is my **stepfather**. He's my mother's second husband.

1 Zack Barry

Gina is my **stepmother**. She's my father's second wife.

Beth Gina

Jim is my **stepbrother**. His mother married my father.

Kayla is my **stepsister**.

2 Kayla Jim

Carl is my **stepson**. I married his father three years ago.

3 Carl Gail

Tina is my **stepdaughter**. I married her mother when Tina was five.

Mike Tina

Dana is my **half-sister**. We have the same mother, but different fathers.*

Rob's my **half-brother**.

4 Rob Dana

*Half-brothers and half-sisters can also have the same father but different mothers.

B Pair work Ask your partner to find people in the photos.

❝ Who's Carl's stepmother? ❞ ❝ Carl's stepmother is Gail. ❞

C 🔊 2:09 **Listening comprehension** Listen to the speakers and infer the relationships. Use the Vocabulary to complete each statement. Listen again if necessary.

1 Her brother has three ....
2 Carol is his ....
3 She calls her .... "Mom."
4 Leo is his ....
5 Hank is her ....

GRAMMAR The simple present tense—information questions: Review

What **do** your in-laws **do**?
Where **do** their grandparents **live**?
When **do** you **visit** your aunt?
How often **do** you **call** your nephew?
How many cousins **do** they **have**?

What **does** your sister-in-law **do**?
Where **does** your niece **live**?
When **does** he **visit** his aunt?
How often **does** she **call** her nephew?
How many cousins **does** he **have**?

Be careful! Who as subject:
Who **lives** in Hong Kong?
NOT Who ~~does live~~ in Hong Kong?

Information questions in the simple present tense:
• Form
• Questions with Who
• Common errors

A Find the grammar Look at the Photo Story on page 27 again. Find one information question in the simple present tense.

B Grammar practice Complete the conversations with the simple present tense.

1 A: .... nieces and nephews
.....................?

B: Three. My sister .... two girls, and my
brother .... a boy.

2 A: My stepfather .... in a restaurant.

B: Really? .... he ....?

A: He's the chef and manager.

3 A: My sister .... with her family in Dublin.

B: Dublin? .... kids .... she have?

A: I have two nephews, both adopted.

4 A: .... your cousins live?

B: One .... in Thailand. And the other
...... in Norway.

A: Wow! .... you see them?

B: They come home once a year.

5 A: Where .... your uncle ....?

B: He .... at the hospital around the corner.

A: .... your aunt .... there, too?

B: No, ... She's a homemaker.

CONVERSATION MODEL

A 🔊 2:10 Read and listen to people describing
their families.

A: Do you come from a large family?

B: Not really. I have two brothers.

A: What about aunts and uncles?

B: Well, I have three aunts on my father's
side. And on my mother's side, I have
two aunts and three uncles.

A: That's pretty big!

B 🔊 2:11 **Rhythm and intonation** Listen
again and repeat. Then practice the
Conversation Model with a partner.

NOW YOU CAN | Describe extended families

A Notepadding List your extended family
relationships on the notepad.

B Pair work Personalize the Conversation
Model. Then change roles.

A: Do you come from a large family?

B: .... I have ....

A: What about ....?

B: Well, I have .... on my .... 's side.
And ....

A: ....

On my father's side . . .	On my mother's side . . .

Don't stop! Ask for more information.
Tell me about your [aunts].
Does she ___? / Do they ___ ?
Is she / Are they [single]?

What ___ ?   Who ___ ?
Where ___ ?   How often ___ ?
When ___ ?   How many ___ ?

C Extension Now tell your classmates about your partner's family.

31

GOAL **Compare people**

BEFORE YOU LISTEN

A 🔊 2:12 **Vocabulary** • *Similarities and differences* Read and listen. Then listen again and repeat.

How are you alike?

We look { **alike.** / **the same.** }   We wear **similar** / We like **the same kind of** } clothes.   **We both** / **Both of us** } like rock music.

How are you different?

We { **don't look alike.** / **look different.** }   We wear / We like } **different** clothes.   I like rock music, **but** { he likes classical. / he doesn't. }

B Pair work Find three similarities and three differences between you and your partner. On a separate sheet of paper, write six sentences describing the similarities and differences.

LISTENING COMPREHENSION

A 🔊 2:13 **Identify similarities and differences** Listen to Lucille Kennedy talk about herself and her sister, Laura. Check the statements that are true. Explain your answers.

Lucille and Laura . . .			
1	☐ look alike.	☐ look different.	
2	☐ like the same food.	☐ like different food.	
3	☐ like the same kinds of movies.	☐ like different kinds of movies.	
4	☐ sometimes wear the same clothes.	☐ never wear the same clothes.	
5	☐ like the same music.	☐ like different music.	
6	☐ have the same number of kids.	☐ have different numbers of kids.	
7	Lucille and Laura are	☐ twins.	☐ stepsisters.	☐ half-sisters.

B ▶)) 2:14 **Listen to take notes** Listen again for what Lucille says about these topics. On your notepad, use the Vocabulary to write sentences about how she and her sister are different.

favorite colors *They like different colors. Lucille likes ...*

favorite colors	sports preferences
musical tastes	families

PRONUNCIATION *Blending sounds*

A ▶)) 2:15 Read and listen. Pay attention to the blended sounds in <u>does she</u> and <u>does he</u>. Then listen again and repeat.

/dʌʃi/
1 Does she have any stepchildren?

/dʌʃi/
2 How many stepchildren does she have?

/dʌzi/
3 Does he live near you?

/dʌzi/
4 Where does he live?

B Now practice the questions on your own. Pay attention to blended sounds.

NOW YOU CAN **Compare people**

A **Notepadding** Choose someone in your extended family. On the notepad, write your similarities and differences. Use the Vocabulary from page 32.

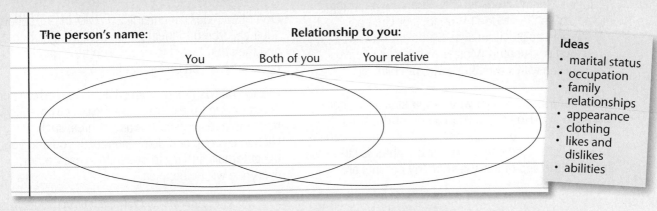

The person's name: _____

Relationship to you: _____

You   Both of you   Your relative

Ideas
• marital status
• occupation
• family relationships
• appearance
• clothing
• likes and dislikes
• abilities

B **Pair work** Tell your partner about you and your relative. Use your notepad. Then compare other people in your families.

" My cousin and I are both single. "

 Be sure to recycle this language.

Similarities and differences	For more information
How are you alike?	How about ___ ?
How are you different?	Do you have any ___ ?
Do you look alike?	How old ___ ?
Do you both ___ ?	What does your ___ do?
Do you ___ the same ___ ?	Where does your ___ live?
	How many ___ does your ___ have?

GOAL **Discuss family cultural traditions**

Warm-up In your opinion, how long should adult children live in their parents' homes?

READING 2:16

Ask Mr. Dad with Armin Brott

Home | About "Ask Mr. Dad" | Ask a Question | About Armin Brott | Visit mrdad.com

When Adult Children Come Home

Q: *My wife and I recently sent our last child off to college. We are ready to sell the house and travel, but our oldest daughter doesn't have a job and plans to move back home. What should we do?*

A: Most North Americans expect their children to move out of the house at eighteen. But that's changing. Today, more adult children are returning home to live. Some don't have jobs or can't pay for the high costs of housing. Some are recently separated or divorced. Most are single, but some come home with a wife, husband, or child, too.

Most parents are happy when their kids come back home to live. However, when a son or daughter can't find a job—or is recently divorced—there can be problems. And if their son or daughter is still at home at the age of thirty-five, many parents are no longer happy.

In your case, what if your daughter moves back home?

• Don't worry. If you and your daughter had a good relationship when she was younger, she'll be fine. Help her in any way you can. And it's OK to ask, "How long do you plan on staying?"

• Don't treat your daughter like a child. In our culture, adult children don't feel good about living at home, and they don't want to depend on their parents' help. Tell her you understand.

• Talk to your daughter as an adult. Have a discussion about paying for expenses and helping with household responsibilities and chores, such as kitchen cleanup and doing laundry. If you and your daughter talk and try to understand each other, everyone will be happier.

Ask Mr. Dad your question at <u>askmrdad.com</u>.

Source: <u>mrdad.com</u>

A Confirm facts Complete each statement.

1 The parents are worried because their daughter ....
   a wants to move into their home   c doesn't want to leave their home
   b wants to move away from their home   d doesn't want to come home

2 According to the article, most North Americans expect children to move out of their parents' home when they ....
   a reach the age of eighteen   c find a job
   b finish college   d get married

B **Infer information** Check all the correct answers, according to what Armin Brott says.

1 Check the reasons adult children are moving
   back home.
   ☐ They don't have jobs.
   ☐ They get divorced.
   ☐ They can't afford housing.
   ☐ They feel good about living with their parents.
   ☐ They want to depend on their parents.

2 What are Mr. Brott's suggestions to the father?
   ☐ to sell his house and go traveling
   ☐ to discuss chores at home
   ☐ to ask his daughter to find a job
   ☐ to try to understand his daughter
   ☐ to not worry too much about his daughter

On your *ActiveBook* Self-Study Disc:
Extra Reading Comprehension Questions

NOW YOU CAN Discuss family cultural traditions

A **Frame your ideas** Complete the survey about adult children in your country. Then compare answers with a partner.

Living At Home?

1 **At what age do children usually leave home in your country?**

☐ between 18 and 20
☐ between 21 and 25
☐ between 26 and 30
☐ over 30
☐ It depends on their marital status.

2 **What are the reasons adult children usually leave home?**

☐ They get a job.
☐ They get married.
☐ They go away to study.
☐ They don't want to depend on their parents.
☐ Other _____

3 **How do parents feel when their adult children are living at home?**

☐ They're very happy.
☐ They're very worried.
☐ They don't think about it.
☐ They don't want them to stay.
☐ Other _____

4 **What do adult children usually do when they live at home?**

☐ They help with the chores.
☐ They help pay for expenses.
☐ They look for a job.
☐ They look for a new place to live.
☐ Other _____

B **Notepadding** Write some similarities and differences between family cultural traditions in your country and those Armin Brott describes.

What's the same?	What's different?

C **Group work** Now imagine that you are speaking to a visitor to your country. Explain the family cultural traditions in your country about adult children living at home.

Text-mining (optional)
Underline language in the Reading on page 34 to use in the Group Work. For example:
"Most parents are happy when ..."

Review

More Practice

ActiveBook Self-Study Disc

grammar · vocabulary · listening
reading · speaking · pronunciation

A 🔊 **Listening comprehension** Listen to the people talking about their families. Check the box for family size for each speaker. Then listen again and write the number of children in each person's family.

		A big family	A small family	Number of children
1	Brenda	☐	☐	
2	Steven	☐	☐	
3	Leslie	☐	☐	
4	Jason	☐	☐	

B Complete the sentences with the correct word or phrase.

1 Larry doesn't have any brothers or sisters. He's an ....

2 Bob's brother is Ron. They have the same birth date. They are ....

3 Jun's brother has two daughters. They are Jun's ....

4 Eva is Alfonso's wife. Alfonso's parents are Eva's ....

5 Hariko's father has five nieces and nephews. They are Hariko's ....

6 Jill's father married Wendy's mother. Jill's father is Wendy's ....

7 Julie and Brett are divorced. Brett is Julie's ....

8 Teresa's mother has two brothers. They are Teresa's ....

C Complete the questions. Use the simple present tense.

1 A: Where ....?
   B: My brother lives in Cuzco, Peru.

2 A: What ....?
   B: My sister's a nurse.

3 A: How many ....?
   B: I have two sons and a daughter.

4 A: ....?
   B: Cousins? Yes, I do. I have seven.

5 A: Where ....?
   B: My brother lives near me.

6 A: ....?
   B: Children? Yes. My sister has two daughters.

D **Writing** On a separate sheet of paper, compare two people in your family. Write about how they are similar and how they are different.

> My brother and his wife are similar in some ways, but they are also very different . . .

2:18/2:19

🎵 **Top Notch Pop**
"An Only Child"
Lyrics p. 149

WRITING BOOSTER ▸ p. 143

• *Combining sentences with and or but*
• *Guidance for Exercise D*

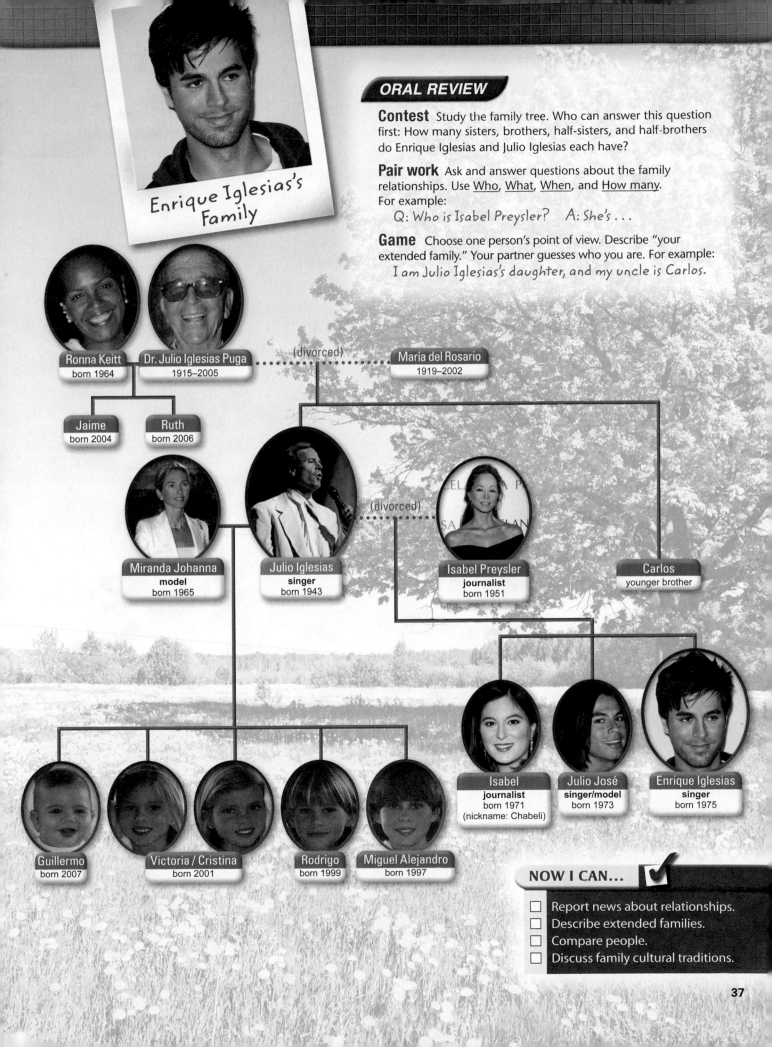

Enrique Iglesias's Family

Contest Study the family tree. Who can answer this question first: How many sisters, brothers, half-sisters, and half-brothers do Enrique Iglesias and Julio Iglesias each have?

Pair work Ask and answer questions about the family relationships. Use <u>Who</u>, <u>What</u>, <u>When</u>, and <u>How many</u>. For example:

Q: Who is Isabel Preysler?   A: She's . . .

Game Choose one person's point of view. Describe "your extended family." Your partner guesses who you are. For example:

I am Julio Iglesias's daughter, and my uncle is Carlos.

Ronna Keitt
born 1964

Dr. Julio Iglesias Puga
1915–2005

(divorced)

María del Rosario
1919–2002

Jaime
born 2004

Ruth
born 2006

Miranda Johanna
model
born 1965

Julio Iglesias
singer
born 1943

(divorced)

Isabel Preysler
journalist
born 1951

Carlos
younger brother

Guillermo
born 2007

Victoria / Cristina
born 2001

Rodrigo
born 1999

Miguel Alejandro
born 1997

Isabel
journalist
born 1971
(nickname: Chabeli)

Julio José
singer/model
born 1973

Enrique Iglesias
singer
born 1975

NOW I CAN... ✓

- ☐ Report news about relationships.
- ☐ Describe extended families.
- ☐ Compare people.
- ☐ Discuss family cultural traditions.

Food and Restaurants

GOALS After Unit 4, you will be able to:
1 Ask for a restaurant recommendation.
2 Order from a menu.
3 Speak to a server and pay for a meal.
4 Discuss food and health.

WORLD CAFÉ

Today's Specials

Appetizers

Potato soup
Colombian Style

*

Fried squid
with spicy tomato sauce

Salads

Mixed green salad

*

Tomato onion salad

Entrées

Brazilian steak

*

Grilled fish

*

Roast chicken

Desserts

Ice cream

*

Apple pie

*

German chocolate cake

Beverages

Coffee * Tea * Soft drinks * Fruit juice * Bottled water (still or sparkling)

A Read the menu. Circle the words that are new to you.

B 🔊 2:20 **Vocabulary • *Parts of a meal*** Listen and repeat.

C **Pair work** Which foods on the menu would you like to order? Are there any foods you wouldn't like to order? Compare tastes with a partner.

D **Notepadding** Write the name of at least one dish from your country for each category.

an appetizer	
a salad	
an entrée (main course)	
a dessert	
a beverage	

E 2:21 🔊 **Photo story** Read and listen to someone ordering food in a restaurant.

ENGLISH FOR TODAY'S WORLD
connecting people from different cultures
and language backgrounds

Server:* Are you ready to order? Or do you need some more time?

Customer: I'm ready, thanks. I think I'll start with the potato soup. Then I'll have the roast chicken. What does that come with?

Server: It comes with a salad. And there's also a choice of vegetables. Tonight we have carrots or grilled tomatoes.

Customer: I'd like the carrots, please. Or, on second thought, maybe I'll have the tomatoes.

Server: Certainly. And anything to drink?

Customer: I'd like sparkling water, please. No ice.

*Server = waiter (man) or waitress (woman)

Server: Portuguese speaker

F **Infer meaning** Check the correct answers.

1 What does the customer order?
☐ an appetizer
☐ an entrée
☐ a dessert
☐ a beverage

2 What does the entrée come with?
☐ soup and salad
☐ salad and dessert
☐ carrots and grilled tomatoes
☐ salad and carrots or grilled tomatoes
☐ water

G **Focus on language** Use the menu from the World Café. Complete each statement.

1 I think I'll start with the ....

2 Then I'll have the ....

3 For my main course, I'd like the ....

4 For dessert, I'll have the ....

5 To drink, I'd like ....

H **Pair work** Read your statements to a partner. Your partner writes your order on the notepad. Then listen to and write your partner's statements.

Guest Check

Date	Table	Server	Check No. 2650

Tax

Total

GOAL **Ask for a restaurant recommendation**

VOCABULARY   *Categories of food*

A 🔊 2:22 Read and listen. Then listen again and repeat. Add another food to each category.

fruit		vegetables		meat		seafood	
① apples	② bananas	⑤ carrots	⑥ peppers	⑨ chicken	⑩ lamb	⑬ fish	⑭ clams
③ grapes	④ oranges	⑦ broccoli	⑧ onions	⑪ sausage	⑫ beef	⑮ shrimp	⑯ crab
mangoes						⑰ squid	

grains		dairy products		oils		sweets	
⑱ pasta	⑲ rice	㉒ butter	㉓ cheese	㉖ corn oil	㉗ olive oil	㉙ candy	㉚ pie
⑳ noodles	㉑ bread	㉔ milk	㉕ yogurt	㉘ coconut oil		㉛ cake	㉜ cookies

B Expand the vocabulary How many foods can you create? Combine foods. Follow the example.

1 orange **juice**   *apple juice, mango juice*

2 tomato onion **salad** ....

3 apple **pie** ....

4 **grilled** fish ....

5 **fried** squid ....

6 potato **soup** ....

GRAMMAR   *There is* and *there are* with count and non-count nouns

Use **there is** with non-count nouns and singular count nouns.
Use **there are** with plural count nouns.

> **There's** milk and an apple in the fridge.
> **There are** oranges, too. But **there aren't** any vegetables.

Use **there is** with **anything** and **nothing**.

> **Is there** anything to eat? (No, **there is** nothing.)
> NOT ~~Are there~~ anything to eat?

GRAMMAR BOOSTER ▸ p. 127

- More on non-count nouns
- Expressing quantities
- *How much* / *how many*
- Spelling rules

Remember:
- Count nouns name things you can count. They are singular or plural.
- Non-count nouns name things you cannot count. They are not singular or plural.
- Don't use <u>a</u>, <u>an</u>, or a number with non-count nouns.
    rice   NOT ~~a rice~~   NOT ~~rices~~

See page 122 for a more complete list of non-count nouns.

Grammar practice Complete each statement or question with a form of <u>there is</u> or <u>there are</u>.

1 .... apples in the fridge?

2 .... any cookies?

3 .... anything to eat in this house? I'm hungry.

4 .... eggs in the fridge. We could make an omelet.

5 I don't think .... any vegetables on the menu.

6 .... too much sugar in this coffee.

7 .... enough lettuce to make a salad?

8 .... any of that great cheese? I feel like having a grilled cheese sandwich.

2:23

CONVERSATION MODEL

A 🔊 Read and listen to someone asking for a restaurant recommendation.

A: Could you recommend a restaurant for this evening?

B: Sure. What are you in the mood for?

A: I don't know. Maybe a sandwich. I'm not very hungry.

B: Actually, there's a great place nearby. It's called Tom's. Would you like directions?

B 🔊 **Rhythm and intonation** Listen and repeat. Then practice the Conversation Model with a partner.

🔊 **Degrees of hunger**
- not very hungry
+ really hungry
+++ starving

NOW YOU CAN Ask for a restaurant recommendation

A Pair work Change the Conversation Model. Ask for a recommendation for today, tonight, dinner, breakfast, or lunch. Recommend a restaurant from the map. Then change roles.

A: Could you recommend a restaurant for ....?

B: .... What are you in the mood for?

A: I don't know. Maybe .... I'm ....

B: Actually, there's a great place nearby. It's called .... Would you like directions?

Don't stop!
Use the map and give directions to the restaurant you recommended.

 Be sure to recycle this language.

Locations	
around the corner	down the street from the ___
across the street	between ___ and ___
across from the ___	on the ___ side of the street

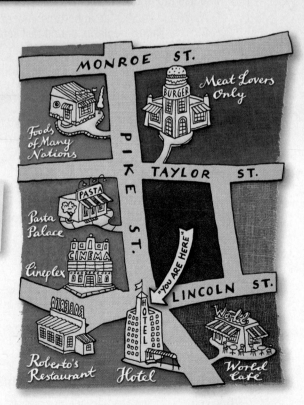

B Change partners Practice the conversation again. Talk about other foods and restaurants.

GOAL   Order from a menu

CONVERSATION MODEL

A 🔊 2:26 Read and listen to someone ordering dinner from a menu.

A: I'll have the pasta for my main course, please. What does that come with?

B: It comes with soup or a salad.

A: What kind of soup is there?

B: There's tomato soup or chicken soup.

A: I'd like the salad, please.

B: Certainly. And to drink?

A: Water, please.

B 🔊 2:27 **Rhythm and intonation** Listen again and repeat. Then practice the Conversation Model with a partner.

GRAMMAR   *Definite article the*

> **Use the definite article <u>the</u> to name something a second time.**
> A: It comes with a salad.
> B: OK. I'll have **the salad**.
>
> **Also use <u>the</u> to talk about something specific.**
> A: Would you like an appetizer? (not specific; general)
> B: Yes. **The fried clams** sound delicious. (specific; they're on the menu)
>
> A: I'm in the mood for seafood. (not specific; general)
> B: Then I recommend **the grilled shrimp**. (also specific; they're on the menu)

> **Remember:**
> The indefinite articles are <u>a</u> and <u>an</u>.
>
> **a** salad   **an** appetizer
> **a** beverage **an** entrée

> **GRAMMAR BOOSTER** ▸ p. 129
> • *Some* and *any*

A Find the grammar Look at the Photo Story on page 39 again. Explain why the customer uses the definite article <u>the</u> in the following sentences.

1 "I think I'll start with <u>the</u> potato soup."   **3** "I'd like <u>the</u> carrots, please."

2 "Then I'll have <u>the</u> roast chicken."   **4** " . . . maybe I'll have <u>the</u> tomatoes."

B Grammar practice Complete each conversation with <u>a</u>, <u>an</u>, or <u>the</u>.

1 A: What do you feel like eating tonight?

   B: Well, ... seafood special sounds delicious.

2 A: I'm in the mood for .... really spicy dish.

   B: Well, what about .... Thai chicken? Thai food is usually spicy.

3 A: There are two kinds of soup: chicken noodle and mixed vegetable.

B: I think I'd like .... chicken noodle. I'm not .... big vegetable fan.

4 A: What would you like for your main course? We have .... nice grilled chicken special on .... menu tonight.

B: That sounds good. I'll have .... chicken special.

PRONUNCIATION   *The*

A 🔊 **2:28** Compare the pronunciation of <u>the</u> before consonant and vowel sounds. Read and listen. Then listen again and repeat.

/ə/ (before consonant sounds)
the chicken
the soup
the juice
the hot appetizer
the fried eggs

/i/ (before vowel sounds)
the orange juice
the onion soup
the apple juice
the appetizer
the eggs

B Write a check mark if the <u>underlined</u> word begins with a vowel sound.

- ☑ the <u>egg</u> salad
- ☐ the <u>Chinese</u> fried squid
- ☐ the <u>tomato</u> sauce
- ☐ the <u>apple</u> cake
- ☐ the <u>ice</u> cream
- ☐ the <u>chocolate</u> milk
- ☐ the <u>clam</u> soup
- ☐ the <u>olive</u> oil
- ☐ the <u>grilled</u> fish

C **Pair work** Now take turns saying each phrase. Be sure to use the correct pronunciation of <u>the</u>.

NOW YOU CAN   Order from a menu

A With a partner, invent a restaurant. Give your restaurant a name. Write foods on the menu. Include two or more choices for each category.

B **Pair work** Use your menu to order food. Pay attention to count and non-count nouns and definite and indefinite articles. Then change roles.

A: I'll have .... for my main course, please. What does that come with?

B: It comes with ....

A: What kind of .... is there?

B: ....

A: I'd like .... , please.

B: Certainly. And to drink?

A: .... , please.

Don't stop!
- Order an appetizer or a soup.
- Order dessert.

C **Extension** Bring in a real menu from your favorite restaurant. Use it to practice the conversation. Change partners and menus and practice again.

Welcome to

_____
(name of restaurant)

appetizers:
_____

soup:
_____

entrées:
_____

beverages:
_____

All entrées come with:
_____

GOAL Speak to a server and pay for a meal

2:29

🔊 **Vocabulary** • *Communicating with a waiter or waitress*
Read and listen. Then listen again and repeat.

Excuse me!

We're ready to order.

I'm sorry. This isn't what I ordered.

We'll take the check, please.

Is the tip included?

Do you accept credit cards?

LISTENING COMPREHENSION

2:30

A 🔊 **Listen to predict** Listen to the conversations in a restaurant. Then listen again and predict the next thing you think the customer will say to the server. Explain your answers.

1 ☐ We'll take the check, please.
   ☐ Do you accept credit cards?
   ☐ We're ready to order.

2 ☐ This isn't what I ordered.
   ☐ We're ready to order.
   ☐ Is the tip included?

3 ☐ No, thanks. We'll take the check, please.
   ☐ Is the tip included?
   ☐ Do you accept credit cards?

4 ☐ Excuse me! This isn't what I ordered.
   ☐ Excuse me! We're ready to order.
   ☐ Excuse me! We'll take the check, please.

5 ☐ Excuse me!
   ☐ We'll start with the seafood soup, please.
   ☐ We'll take the check, please.

B **Pair work** Decide what to say to the server in each conversation. Then practice the conversation.

1 A: Oh, no! Have a look at this check!

   B: I'm not sure we have enough money.
      Excuse me! ....*Do you accept credit cards?*....

2 A: Oh, no! They brought us onion soup.
      We ordered the tomato soup.

   B: You're right. Excuse me! ....

3 A: Oh, no! I left my money at home.

    B: Excuse me! ....

4 A: We can't order dessert. We don't have time.

    B: Right. Excuse me! ....

5 A: Do we need to leave a tip?

    B: I'll ask. Excuse me! ....

6 A: Where's the waitress? I'm starving.

    B: Excuse me! ....

NOW YOU CAN   Speak to a server and pay for a meal

A **Notepadding** Plan your meal. Read the menu and choose what you'd like to order. Write your choice for each category.

appetizer	
soup	
salad	
main course	
beverage	
dessert	

Parkview Restaurant

Appetizers

Crab cakes

Mini cheese pies

Mixed grilled vegetables

Soup

Spicy shrimp

Chicken and rice

French onion

Salads

Tomato pepper

Green bean

Carrot

Entrées

Roast beef

Fried fish

Pasta with clam sauce

Choice of Vegetables: Broccoli, Grilled tomatoes, Potatoes (any style)

Desserts

Ice cream sandwiches

Banana cake

Chocolate pie

Mixed fruit salad

Fruit and cheese plate

All entrées include bread, soup or salad, vegetable, coffee or tea

B **Group work** Now form groups of diners and servers at tables. Discuss the menu. Speak to the server. Order and pay for the meal.

♻ **Be sure to recycle this language.**

Discuss food	Serve food	Order food	Pay for food
What are you in the mood for?	Are you ready to order?	Excuse me!	I'll / We'll take the check, please.
I'm in the mood for ___ .	Do you need more time?	I'm / We're ready.	Is the tip included?
There's ___ on the menu.	That comes with ___ .	I'd like to start with ___ .	Do you accept credit cards?
The ___ sound(s) delicious.	Would you like ___ ?	I think I'll have ___ .	
What about ___ ?	Anything to drink?	And then I'll have ___ .	
This isn't what I ordered.	And to drink?	Does that come with ___ ?	
	And for your [entrée]?	What does that come with?	
		What kind of ___ is there?	

45

GOAL   Discuss food and health

A 2:31 **Vocabulary** • *Adjectives to describe the healthfulness of food* Read and listen. Then listen again and repeat.

healthy / healthful   is good for you

unhealthy / unhealthful   is bad for you

fatty / high-fat   contains a lot of oil

salty   contains a lot of salt

sweet   contains a lot of sugar

high-calorie   can make you fat or overweight

low-calorie   is not going to make you fat

B Warm-up Do you like to eat at fast-food restaurants? Is it possible to get healthy food there? Use the Vocabulary.

READING 2:32

| File | Edit | View | History | Bookmarks | Tools | Help |

Get Smart! Eating on the go

| Home | Eating on the go |

Eat more "veggies."

We know a daily diet of fast food can be bad for us. But fast food is quick and easy, and when we're on the go, it's sometimes a necessary choice. So here are some tips for fast-food fans:

- **Choose the chicken.** Have chicken rather than red meat. When in doubt, order the grilled chicken—not the fried.

- **Go light on the sauce.** Mayo, salad dressings, and other sauces are loaded with calories. Cut down on them, or cut them out altogether!

Cut down on mayo.

- **Fill up on veggies.** Ask for tomato, lettuce, onion, or other veggies on your sandwich. These low-calorie choices can help you avoid fries and other high-calorie options.

Skip the fries.

- **Go for the regular size,** not the extra-large. Super-size portions can super-size YOU.

- **Skip the sides entirely.** Eating a burger by itself is often enough. If you need a side order of something, consider a fruit cup or a side salad, instead of those fatty, salty french fries. Most fast-food restaurants offer those healthy options now.

Get a side salad.

- **Finally, treat yourself.** When you just have to have something sweet, opt for some delicious low-fat frozen yogurt or fruit ices rather than ice cream or cookies. You won't miss the calories a bit!

Source: fruitsandveggiesmatter.gov

A Understand from context Find the following words and phrases in the Reading and match them with their meanings. Then, on a separate sheet of paper, use the words to write your own sentences.

.... 1 "veggies"
.... 2 "side order"
.... 3 "go for"
.... 4 "skip" or "avoid"
.... 5 "portion"
.... 6 "option"

a the amount you eat at one time
b not choose
c vegetables
d choice
e something you eat with your main course
f choose

B Infer information Which tips on the website can help you cut down on calories? fat? salt? sugar? Explain how.

> On your *ActiveBook* Self-Study Disk:
> **Extra Reading Comprehension Questions**

NOW YOU CAN   Discuss food and health

A Frame your ideas Write a ✓ next to the foods you think are healthy. Write an ✗ next to the foods you think are not. Then discuss your answers with a partner. Explain why some of the foods are unhealthy.

> " French fries are not healthy. They're too fatty. "
>
> " I agree. "

☐ rice   ☐ french fries   ☐ hot peppers   ☐ ice cream

☐ snacks: nuts, chips   ☐ chicken   ☐ salad   ☐ pasta with sauce

B Notepadding List other foods and drinks you think are good for you and bad for you.

Healthy foods	Unhealthy foods
oranges	salty foods, like potato chips

C Discussion Now discuss food and health with your class. Suggest healthy eating tips. Use your lists.

> **Text-mining** (optional)
> Underline more language in the Reading on page 46 to use in the Discussion. For example:
> "Have ___ rather than ___ ."

♻ **Be sure to recycle this language.**

Categories of foods		Adjectives	Verbs
grains	meat	healthy / unhealthy	skip / avoid / cut out
seafood	sweets	good / bad for you	go light on / cut down on
dairy products	fruit	high-calorie / low-calorie	fill up on
vegetables	oils	fatty / salty / sweet / spicy	

Review

A 2:33 **Listening comprehension** Listen to the conversations. Where are the people? Choose <u>at home</u> or <u>in a restaurant</u>. Then predict what each person will say next. Listen again and complete the statements.

1 The man and woman are (at home / in a restaurant).
I think he's going to ask, "Does dessert .... with my ....?"

2 Caroline and her mom are (at home / in a restaurant).
Her mom is probably going to say, "But Caroline, ... are really ...."

3 The man and woman are (at home / in a restaurant).
It's possible that he's going to say, "...................... the grilled ...."

4 The couple is (at home / in a restaurant).
It's possible that she's going to say, "Terrific! Let's .... an omelet and a salad. I'm really ....!"

B Write examples of foods for each description below.

Spicy foods	Salty foods	Sweet foods	Fatty foods

C Write four questions you can ask a waiter or a waitress.

1 ....

2 ....

3 ....

4 ....

2:34/2:35
Top Notch Pop
"The World Café"
Lyrics p. 149

D Complete each sentence with a form of <u>there is</u> or <u>there are</u>.

1 .... too much pepper in the soup.

2 I hope .... not too much sugar in the cake. Sugar isn't good for you.

3 Excuse me. I'm looking for a restaurant. .... any good restaurants in the neighborhood?

4 .... any low-fat desserts on the menu?

5 .... an inexpensive restaurant nearby?

6 You should eat some fruit. .... some nice oranges on the kitchen table.

7 .... enough cheese in the fridge for two sandwiches?

8 I'm in the mood for soup. What kind of soup .... on the menu?

E **Writing** On a separate sheet of paper, write a short article for a travel newsletter. Write at least five sentences about foods in your country. Write more if you can.

In my country we eat a lot of vegetables. Vegetable soup is a very typical appetizer . . .

WRITING BOOSTER ▸ p. 143

• Connecting words and ideas: <u>and, in addition</u>
• Guidance for Exercise E

ORAL REVIEW

Pair work Create conversations for the people in Pictures 1, 2, and 3. For example:

A: Can I help you?

B: Could you recommend a restaurant for . . . ?

Contest Form teams. Each team takes turns making statements about the foods in Picture 4 with <u>there is</u> or <u>there are.</u> (Teams get one point for each correct statement.)

NOW I CAN... ✔

- ☐ Ask for a restaurant recommendation.
- ☐ Order from a menu.
- ☐ Speak to a server and pay for a meal.
- ☐ Discuss food and health.

49

Technology and You

All prices in U.S. dollars • No tax if you buy at the airport

AE
AIRPORT ELECTRONICS
Your airport electronics center

Laptop and Desktop Computers
All brands and models
Prices you won't believe!

Blue Dot Bluetooth® Earphone

$32.99
Reg $39.99

For any Bluetooth® v2.0 compatible device

My Buddy 266T Portable GPS
with touch screen free live traffic updates

$299.99

Arch K2R Blu-ray Disc/DVD Player
$279.00

Was $399.00
Save $120.00

Flash Drives, USB Drives, Pen Drives, Memory Sticks, Thumb Drives . . .
Whatever you call 'em, we have 'em!

1GB $3.99 2GB $6.99
4GB $12.99
ALL BRANDS AT ONE LOW, LOW PRICE

Simplex Supershot Digital Camera
10MP 3X optical zoom

Log on to airportelectronics.com for price.

Our price is too low to advertise!

Glimpko Stereo Headphones
$99.99
Micro Black

At this price, you can afford to upgrade!
Buy the headphones and get a free pair of MP3 earbuds!

Stryker 8900X Home Theater LCD Projector
Reg $2,699.99

Log on to airportelectronics.com for sale price.

Low, low price!

Doby 8GB Video MP3 Player
$299.00

Sedgewick ML-506 Camcorder
$499.00

Imitek Speakers
$29.99

Super Special!

USB 2.0

A 🔊 3:02 **Vocabulary • *Electronics*** Listen and repeat.

a laptop (computer)	a digital camera
a desktop (computer)	headphones
an earphone	a projector
a GPS	an MP3 player
a DVD player	a camcorder
a flash drive	speakers

B **Discussion** Choose a product from the ad that you would like in order to replace an old one. Discuss the reasons. Use this vocabulary or your own ideas.

🔊 3:03 **Replacing products**
broken doesn't work
obsolete hard to use because the technology is old
up-to-date uses new or recent technology
defective not good; badly designed and/or manufactured

C 🔊)) **Photo story** Read and listen to a conversation about a product that's not working.

Don: This printer's driving me crazy! It's on the blink again.

Erin: What's wrong with it?

Don: What <u>isn't</u> wrong with it? It's an absolute lemon.

Erin: No, seriously, what's the problem?

Don: Well, first off, the thing's an antique. It's ten years old.

Erin: OK. And . . . ?

Don: And it's <u>so</u> slow. It takes hours to print! And now it won't print at all!

Erin: Well, that <u>is</u> a problem. Maybe it's fixable. Let me have a look.

Don: Don't bother. It's not worth it. The thing's obsolete, anyway. It's not wireless, it has no scanner, it can't photocopy . . .

Erin: Sounds like you're ready for an upgrade. Airport Electronics is having a sale. Let's get you something more up-to-date!

D **Focus on language** Find the following sentences and phrases in the Photo Story. Choose the statement that is closer in meaning to each sentence.

1 "This printer's driving me crazy!"
   a I love this printer!
   b I hate this printer!

2 "It's on the blink again."
   a The printer has a problem.
   b The printer is OK.

3 "It's an absolute lemon."
   a It's very bad.
   b It's very good.

4 ". . . the thing's an antique."
   a It's very new.
   b It's very old.

5 "Don't bother. It's not worth it."
   a I don't want to fix the printer.
   b I want to fix the printer.

6 ". . . you're ready for an upgrade."
   a You need a new printer.
   b Someone needs to fix your printer.

E **Pair work** Make a list of five electronic products that are necessary for your life. Put them in order from most important (1) to least important (5). Compare lists with a partner. Explain why each product is necessary for you.

> ❝I can't live without a laptop. I use it at work and at home . . .❞

	Product	Why necessary?
1		
2		
3		
4		
5		

GOAL Suggest a brand or model

CONVERSATION MODEL

A 🔊 **3:05** Read and listen to someone suggesting a brand and a model.

A: Hey, Lisa. What are you doing?

B: I'm online. I'm looking for a flat screen TV. Any suggestions?

A: What about a Clarion? I hear the LP 10 is great. And it's inexpensive.

B: Really?

A: Yes. You know, I'm going shopping later. Would you like to come along?

🔊 **3:07 Positive descriptions**
pretty good ☺
great ☺☺
terrific ☺☺☺
awesome ☺☺☺☺

B 🔊 **3:06** **Rhythm and intonation** Listen again and repeat. Then practice the Conversation Model with a partner.

GRAMMAR   *The present continuous: Review*

Use the present continuous for actions in progress now and for future plans.

Actions in progress
A: What **are** you **doing** right now?
B: I**'m looking** for a laptop.

Future plans
A: What **are** you **doing** tomorrow?
B: I**'m buying** a digital camera.

Questions
Are you **looking** for a cell phone? (Yes, I am. / No, I'm not.)
Are they **buying** a GPS? (Yes, they are. / No, they're not.)
Is he **using** the computer? (Yes, he is. / No, he's not.)
Where **are** you **going**? (To Technoland.)
Who**'s buying** the new cell phone? (My wife.)

GRAMMAR BOOSTER ▸ p. 130
The present continuous:
• *Spelling rules*
• *Form and usage rules*

Understand the grammar Write <u>now</u> next to the statements or questions where the present continuous describes an action in progress. Write <u>future</u> next to those that describe a future plan.

.... **1** What <u>are</u> you <u>doing</u> this weekend?

.... **2** I'm busy this morning. I<u>'m answering</u> e-mails.

.... **3** He<u>'s leaving</u> in ten minutes. Hurry!

.... **4** Josh isn't home. He<u>'s shopping</u> for a laptop.

.... **5** They<u>'re eating</u> with us on Friday.

.... **6** The printer<u>'s not working</u> again.

PRONUNCIATION   *Intonation of questions*

🔊 **3:08** Listen and check for rising or falling intonation. Then take turns saying each question.

↗ ↘ ☐ ☐ **1** What are you doing?

↗ ↘ ☐ ☐ **2** Are you buying a computer?

↗ ↘ ☐ ☐ **3** What time are you going?

↗ ↘ ☐ ☐ **4** Is she looking for a new printer?

A 🔊 *3:09* Read and listen. Then listen again and repeat.

a smart phone   a cell phone /   a scanner   a photocopier   a fax machine
                   a mobile phone

B Integrated practice Complete each conversation with an electronic product from pages 50–53 and the present continuous.

1 A: .... to Electronica tomorrow?
Marian / go

B: Yes. .... for a new ....
she / shop
The old one is broken, and she listens to music while she's exercising.

2 A: Why .... a ....?
Ann / get

B: She sends a lot of e-mails to her friends, and
....
her old one / not work

3 A: Can I use your ....?

B: Sure. But just a minute. Right now ....
I / use
it to move a file from my laptop to my desktop.

4 A: .... a new presentation, and
Sue / prepare
she wants to use these pictures.

B: She's welcome to use my ....
It's really great.

5 A: Is it possible to use your .... for my
son's birthday party?

B: Sure. What day? .... it tomorrow at
I / use
the school play. After that, you can have it.

6 A: What ....?
your parents / watch

B: A music video. Now that they have a
........................., they watch all day!

NOW YOU CAN Suggest a brand or model

A Pair work Change the Conversation Model, using these ads or ads from a newspaper or online store. Then change roles.

A: I'm looking for .... Any suggestions?

B: What about .... ? I hear the .... is .... And it's ....

A: Really?

B: Yes. You know, I'm going shopping .... Would you like to come along?

♻ **Be sure to recycle this language.**

Are you free ___ ?
I'd love to go, but I ___ .
I'm sorry, but I'm not free ___ .

Don't stop!
Accept or decline the invitation.

B Change partners Discuss other products and suggest other brands or models.

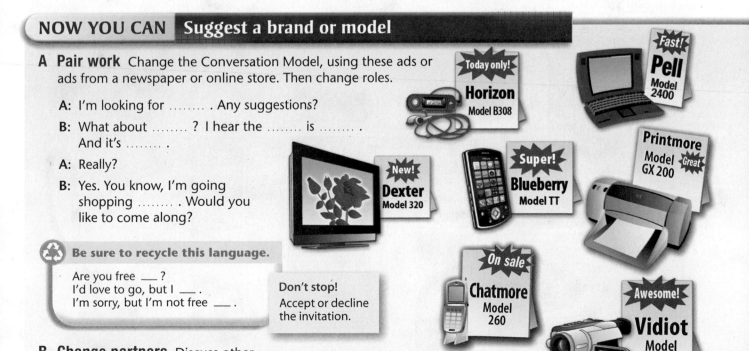

Today only! **Horizon** Model B308

Fast! **Pell** Model 2400

New! **Dexter** Model 320

Super! **Blueberry** Model TT

Printmore Model GX 200 Great

On sale **Chatmore** Model 260

Awesome! **Vidiot** Model XOX

GOAL Express frustration and sympathy

CONVERSATION MODEL

A 🔊 3:10 Read and listen to people expressing frustration and sympathy.

A: Hi, Ed. How's it going?

B: Fine, thanks. But my microwave's not working again.

A: Again? I'm sorry to hear that. What brand is it?

B: A Quickpoint. It's a piece of junk.

B 🔊 3:11 **Rhythm and intonation** Listen again and repeat. Then practice the Conversation Model with a partner.

🔊 3:12 **Ways to sympathize**
I'm sorry to hear that.
That's too bad.
That's a shame.
Oh, no!

🔊 3:13 **Negative descriptions**
a piece of junk   awful
pretty bad   horrible
terrible   a lemon

VOCABULARY *Household appliances and machines*

A 🔊 3:14 Read and listen. Then listen again and repeat.

1 a food processor

2 a hair dryer

3 a pressure cooker

4 a dishwasher

5 a coffee maker

6 a rice cooker

7 a fan

8 a stove   9 an oven

10 a juicer

11 a washing machine
12 a dryer

13 a blender

14 a freezer
15 a refrigerator / a fridge

16 an air-conditioner

17 a vacuum cleaner

B Classify the Vocabulary by purpose. Write examples of appliances in each category.

For cleaning or washing	For food preparation	For cooking	For storage

C 🔊 **Listen to predict** Listen and write the name of the appliance. Then listen again and predict what the other person will say. Check the box.

1 appliance: ....
☐ Is it fixable?
☐ Sure. No problem.

2 appliance: ....
☐ It's an air-conditioner.
☐ It's a Cool Wave.

3 appliance: ....
☐ It's not working? That's a shame.
☐ About thirty, I think.

4 appliance: ....
☐ Oops! Sorry about that.
☐ Sounds great!

5 appliance: ....
☐ Just use a little more water.
☐ I think the machine is defective.

6 appliance: ....
☐ Yeah. I'm so glad I bought it!
☐ I think it's time for an upgrade.

7 appliance: ....
☐ It's a lemon.
☐ Wow. That sounds great.

8 appliance: ....
☐ I'm sorry to hear that.
☐ Sure. Just a second.

NOW YOU CAN | **Express frustration and sympathy**

A Notepadding Think of five products and brands that don't work well. Write them on the notepad.

	Product	Brand
1	a hair dryer	Beautiful Hair

	Product	Brand
1		
2		
3		
4		
5		

B Pair work Change the Conversation Model. Use your own products and brands. Express frustration and sympathy. Use the negative descriptions vocabulary from page 54. Then change roles.

A: Hi, ... How's it going?

B: .... But my ....'s not working again.

A: Again? .... What brand is it?

B: .... It's ....

C Change partners Express frustration about other products and brands.

BEFORE YOU READ

Warm-up What kinds of features are important to you in a new product?

READING 3:16

PRO MUSICA

More than a radio, more than a CD player, more than an MP3 player—the Pro Musica is the first complete music system for your entire life. The innovative, all-in-one Pro Musica fills all the rooms of your house with beautiful music from just one source.

It replaces everything else you listen to. MP3 players, radios, and CD players are a thing of the past. And the whole family can be listening to their favorite music in every room at the same time.

Program the Pro Musica to play Metallica in the kitchen and Brahms in the bedroom. Listen with the portable wireless speakers or on your innovative wireless earbuds. You and your spouse can even be listening to two different things in the very same room at the same time. The sky's the limit!

And even better—you can take the Pro Musica's remote and wireless speakers with you anywhere—to the office, to your friend's house for a party, or even to the beach. Play anything, anywhere.

The Pro Musica wireless remote—
Battery operated and easy to use.

The Pro Musica wireless speakers—
Place them anywhere.

The Pro Musica wireless earbuds—
Move around as you listen.

FEATURES

◆ **IT'S CONVENIENT.** Everything you need is built into the system so you can enjoy your music all from one source—and with only one simple-to-use remote control.

◆ **IT'S POPULAR.** The Pro Musica is now used by more households than any other home music system.

◆ **IT'S PORTABLE.** The remote is small and easy to carry. It comes with its own battery pack, so you can take it with you anywhere.

◆ **IT'S AFFORDABLE.** One Pro Musica system costs much less than the many CD players, radios, etc. that most people have to buy to have music in their lives.

◆ **IT'S GUARANTEED.** Use Pro Musica for a full year. If for any reason you are unhappy with the product, just return it for a full refund.

A Understand from context Choose one of the features to complete each statement.

1 A product that's easy to move from one place to another is ....
2 A product that's easy to use is ....
3 A product that you can send back to the store because you don't like it is ....
4 A product that a lot of people like and buy is ....
5 A product that doesn't cost too much for most people is ....

Features
guaranteed
popular
portable
affordable
convenient

B Activate language from a text Would you buy the Pro Musica? Explain your answer. Use the features vocabulary and your own ideas.

C 🔊 **Listening comprehension** Listen to the radio advertisements for some crazy gadgets. Check all the adjectives that describe each product.

gadget /'gædʒɪt/ n.
a small tool or machine that makes a particular job easier

Longman Dictionary of American English

1 "The Sleeper"

☐ convenient ☐ popular
☐ portable ☐ affordable

2 "Cool as a Cucumber"

☐ convenient ☐ popular
☐ portable ☐ affordable

3 "The Scribbler"

☐ guaranteed ☐ convenient
☐ affordable ☐ popular

D 🔊 **Pair work** Choose one of the three gadgets. Listen again and take notes on a separate sheet of paper. Then try to convince your partner to buy the product. Use the features vocabulary from the Reading on page 56.

On your *ActiveBook* Self-Study Disc:
Extra Reading Comprehension Questions

NOW YOU CAN Describe features of products

A Notepadding Choose one good product that you own and one bad product (appliances, electronic products, gadgets, etc.). Write the good and bad features on the notepad.

Product	Brand	Features
scanner	Blue Bird	obsolete
MP3 player	Vista	affordable / up-to-date

Product	Brand	Features

B Discussion Describe the features of your products. Tell your classmates about all the good and bad features.

❝I don't recommend the Blue Bird scanner. It's obsolete.❞

❝You should buy the new Vista MP3 player. It's affordable and up-to-date.❞

♻ **Be sure to recycle this language.**

Negative descriptions		Positive descriptions		Ways to sympathize
awful	slow	great	guaranteed	I'm sorry to hear that.
broken	terrible	terrific	affordable	That's too bad.
defective	an antique	awesome	convenient	That's a shame.
horrible	a lemon	fast	pretty good	Oh, no!
not fixable	a piece of junk	popular	up-to-date	Maybe it's fixable.
obsolete	drives me crazy			You're ready for an upgrade.
on the blink				

GOAL **Complain when things don't work**

A 🔊 3:19 **Vocabulary • *Ways to state a problem*** Read and listen. Then listen again and repeat.

The window **won't open / close**.

The iron **won't turn on**.

The air-conditioning **won't turn off**.

The fridge is **making a funny sound**.

The toilet **won't flush**.

The sink **is clogged**.

B Write the names of machines, appliances, and gadgets that sometimes . . .

1 won't open or close. ....

2 won't turn on or off. ....

3 make a funny sound. ....

A 🔊 3:20 **Listen for details** Listen to the conversations. Write the room number for each complaint. Then listen again and write another problem for each room.

GUEST COMPLAINT LOG

ROOM	PROBLEM	OTHER PROBLEMS?
203	The toilet won't stop flushing.	
	The fridge isn't working.	
	The sink is clogged.	

B Discussion Which problems on the guest complaint log are serious? Which are not serious? Explain your reasons.

> It's serious when the sink is clogged. Water on the floor is very bad.

NOW YOU CAN | Complain when things don't work

A Notepadding Find and circle all the problems in the hotel. Write the problems on the notepad.

Room / place	Problem(s)

B Pair work Create conversations between the hotel guests and the front desk clerk. Based on the pictures, complain about things that don't work.

> Hello. Front desk. Can I help you?

> I'm in the elevator. It's not working.

> I'll send someone right away.

 Be sure to recycle this language.

Telephone language
Hello?
This is room ___ .
Can I call you back?
Bye.

State a problem
___ won't open / close.
___ won't turn on / off.
___ won't flush / stop flushing.
___ isn't working.
___ is clogged.
___ is making a funny sound.
___ is driving me crazy.

Respond
What's the problem?
I'm sorry to hear that.
Oh, no!
Well, that is a problem.

Review

A ◀)) **Listening comprehension** Listen to the conversations about
problems with products and appliances. Write a sentence to describe
each problem.

Example: *The fan won't turn on.*

1 ....

2 ....

3 ....

4 ....

3:22/3:23
Top Notch Pop
"It's Not Working Again"
Lyrics p. 149

B Complete each conversation with a question in the present continuous.
(It's possible to write more than one question.)

1 A: Where .... tomorrow?

B: We're going to My Electronics World.
Want to come along?

2 A: Are you .... a new
camera?

B: Yes. Our old camera is obsolete. It's
not digital.

3 A: When ....?

B: He's getting a smart phone for his
birthday.

4 A: What ....?

B: Tomorrow? We're fixing our old printer.

5 A: What ....?

B: Right now? We're eating dinner.

C Complete each statement. Circle the correct word or phrase.

1 This new toilet is (defective / portable). It doesn't flush.

2 I think my TV is (affordable / broken). I hope it's fixable.

3 Your computer is probably (obsolete / up-to-date). You should get a new one.

4 This scanner is really a piece of junk. I think we should get (an upgrade / a lemon).

D Classify products, appliances, and gadgets on the following chart. Write at least three in each category.
(Some products may go in more than one category.)

Machines that are:						
Portable	Popular	Convenient	Affordable	Good for communication	Good for entertainment	Good for cooking
					MP3 player	

E **Writing** On a separate sheet of paper, write a paragraph
describing a product, appliance, or gadget that you use.
It can be a good product or a bad one.

I have a Hot Spot dishwasher and . . .

WRITING BOOSTER ▸ p. 144

• *Placement of adjectives*
• *Guidance for Exercise E*

Contest Form teams. Study the pictures for two minutes. Then close your books. Ask another team questions about each picture.
(One point for each correct answer.) For example:
  Q: Is there a hair dryer in the kitchen?
  A: Yes, there is.

Pair work
1 Point at the people and ask and answer questions. Use the present continuous. For example:
  Q: What's he doing?
  A: He's listening to music on his MP3 player.
2 Create conversations for the people in Pictures 1, 2, and 4. For example:
  A: The vacuum cleaner's not working again.
  B: Again? I'm sure it's fixable.

Quickpix 200
$129.99

Techno 100
$699.99

NOW I CAN...
☐ Suggest a brand or model.
☐ Express frustration and sympathy.
☐ Describe features of products.
☐ Complain when things don't work.

Staying in Shape

GOALS   After Unit 6, you will be able to

1 Plan an activity with someone.
2 Talk about habitual activities.
3 Discuss fitness and eating habits.
4 Describe someone's routines.

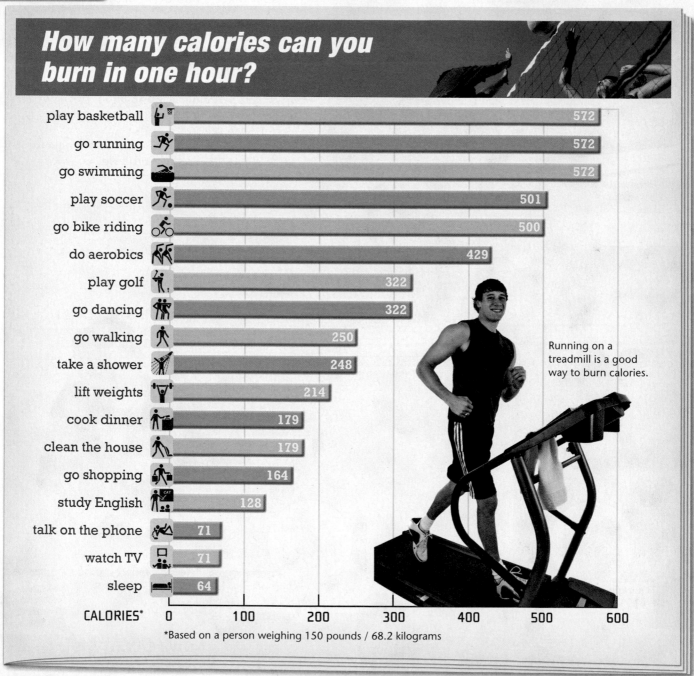

How many calories can you burn in one hour?

Activity	Calories
play basketball	572
go running	572
go swimming	572
play soccer	501
go bike riding	500
do aerobics	429
play golf	322
go dancing	322
go walking	250
take a shower	248
lift weights	214
cook dinner	179
clean the house	179
go shopping	164
study English	128
talk on the phone	71
watch TV	71
sleep	64

CALORIES*   0   100   200   300   400   500   600

*Based on a person weighing 150 pounds / 68.2 kilograms

Running on a treadmill is a good way to burn calories.

Source: msnbc.com

A ◀))) **Vocabulary • *Activities*** Listen and repeat.
^{3:24}

B **Class survey** According to the graph, approximately how many calories do you burn every day? Find out who in your class burns more than 1500 calories a day.

C 🔊 3:25 **Photo story** Read and listen to people talking about playing tennis.

Lynn: Hi, Joy! What are you up to?

Joy: Lynn! How are you? I'm playing tennis, actually. In the park.

Lynn: You play tennis? I didn't know that.

Joy: I do. About three times a week. Do you play?

Lynn: Not as much as I'd like to.

Joy: Well, why don't we make a date to play sometime?

Lynn: That would be great.

Joy: Hey, how about your husband? Would he like to come, too?

Lynn: No way. Ken's a real couch potato. He just watches TV and eats junk food. He's so out of shape.

Joy: Too bad. My husband's crazy about tennis.

Lynn: Listen. I'm on my way home right now. Let's talk next week. OK?

Joy: Terrific.

D **Focus on language** Look at the underlined expressions in the Photo Story. Use the context to help you choose the correct meaning of the following sentences.

1 What are you up to?
  a What are you doing?
  b Where are you going?

2 Why don't we play tennis sometime?
  a Can you explain why we don't play tennis?
  b Would you like to play tennis sometime?

3 My husband is really out of shape.
  a My husband doesn't exercise.
  b My husband exercises a lot.

4 I'm crazy about tennis.
  a I hate tennis.
  b I love tennis.

E **Personalize** Review time expressions. Look at page 62. List the activities you do . . .

every day	every weekend	once a week	once in a while	never

F **Pair work** Compare activities with a partner.

“ What do you do every weekend? ”

“ Me? I go shopping. ”

GOAL   Plan an activity with someone

GRAMMAR   _Can_ and _have to_

can

Use can + the base form of a verb for possibility.

I **can go** out for dinner tonight. I don't have class in the morning.
I **can't play** golf today. I'm too busy.
She **can meet** us at the park, but her husband **can't**.
Can you **go** running tomorrow at three? (Yes, I can. / No, I can't.)

> **Remember:** can + base form also expresses ability.
> We **can speak** English.
> They **can't play** piano.

have to

Use have to or has to + the base form of a verb for obligation.

She { has to / doesn't have to } meet her cousin at the airport.

They { have to / don't have to } work late tonight.

Do you **have to work** tomorrow? (Yes, I do. / No, I don't.)
Does he **have to go** to class? (Yes, he does. / No, he doesn't.)

> **Usage:** When declining an invitation, use _have to_ to provide a reason.
> Sorry, I **can't**. I **have to work** late.

> **GRAMMAR BOOSTER** ▸ p. 131
> _Can_ and _have to:_
> • _Form and common errors_
> • _Information questions_
> _Can_ and _be able to:_
> • _Present and past forms_

A Grammar practice Read the sentences carefully. Then complete each sentence with _can_ or _have to_.

1 I'd like to go out tonight, but we have a test tomorrow. I ....
   _{study}

2 Audrey .... us for lunch today. She .... her boss write a report.
   _{not / meet}   _{help}

3 Good news! I .... late tonight. We .... together at 6:00.
   _{not / work}   _{go running}

4 My sister .... at the mall today. She .... to the doctor.
   _{not / go shopping}   _{go}

5 Henry .... to Toronto next week, so he .... golf with us.
   _{go}   _{not / play}

B Pair work On a separate sheet of paper, write three questions using _can_ and three questions using _have to_. Then practice asking and answering the questions with a partner.

PRONUNCIATION   _Can / can't_

A 🔊 3:26 Listen to the pronunciation and stress of _can_ and _can't_ in sentences. Then listen again and repeat.

I can **call** you today.   I **can't** call you tomorrow.

/kən/   /kænt/

B 🔊 3:27 Listen to the statements and check _can_ or _can't_. Then listen again and repeat each statement.

1 ☐ can   ☐ can't   3 ☐ can   ☐ can't   5 ☐ can   ☐ can't
2 ☐ can   ☐ can't   4 ☐ can   ☐ can't   6 ☐ can   ☐ can't

A 🔊 3:28 Read and listen to two people planning an activity together.

A: Hey, Phil. Why don't we go bike riding sometime?

B: Great idea. When's good for you?

A: Tomorrow at 3:00?

B: Sorry, I can't. I have to meet my sister at the airport.

A: Well, how about Sunday afternoon at 2:00?

B: That sounds fine. See you then.

B 🔊 3:29 **Rhythm and intonation** Listen again and repeat. Then practice the Conversation Model with a partner.

NOW YOU CAN Plan an activity with someone

A Write your schedule for this weekend in the daily planner.

	Friday	Saturday	Sunday
9:00	go running	visit Mom	

Daily Planner

	Friday	Saturday	Sunday
9:00			
11:00			
1:00			
3:00			
5:00			
7:00			

B **Pair work** Now change the Conversation Model, using your daily planner. Then change roles.

A: Hey, ... Why don't we .... sometime?

B: .... When's good for you?

A: ....?

B: Sorry, I can't. I have to ....

A: Well, how about ....?

B: ....

Don't stop!
• Make more excuses using can't and have to.
• Suggest other activities you can do together. (Use page 62 for ideas.)
• Discuss where to meet.

C **Change partners** Plan other activities. Use your daily planner to respond.

GOAL **Talk about habitual activities**

A ◀)) 3:30 Read and listen. Then listen again and repeat.

a park

a gym

a track

a pool

an athletic field

a golf course

a tennis court

B Pair work Tell your partner what you do at these places.

> 66 I play soccer at the athletic field next to the school. 99

GRAMMAR *The present continuous and the simple present tense: Review*

The present continuous	**The simple present tense**
(for actions in progress and future plans)	(for frequency, habits, and routines)
I'm **making** dinner right now.	I **make** dinner at least twice a week.
They're **swimming** at the pool in the park.	They usually **swim** at the pool on Tuesdays.
He's **meeting** his friends for lunch tomorrow.	He hardly ever **meets** his friends for dinner.

Be careful!

Don't use the present continuous with frequency adverbs.

Don't say: ~~She's never playing tennis.~~

Don't use the present continuous with <u>have</u>, <u>want</u>, <u>need</u>, or <u>like</u>.

Don't say: ~~She's liking the gym.~~

GRAMMAR BOOSTER ▸ p. 133

• *Non-action verbs*
• *Placement of frequency adverbs*
• *Time expressions*

◀)) 3:31 **Frequency adverbs**

100% always
almost always
usually / often / generally
sometimes / occasionally
hardly ever
0% never

A Grammar practice Complete the sentences. Use the simple present tense or the present continuous.

1 Brian can't answer the phone right now.
   ....
   He / study

2 How often .... walking?
   she / go

3 .... tennis this weekend.
   We / play

4 .... weights three times a week.
   He / lift

5 .... lunch. Can they call you back?
   They / make

6 How often .... the house?
   you / clean

7 .... aerobics every day.
   I / do

8 .... shopping tonight.
   She / go

B 🔊 **Listening comprehension** Listen to the conversations. Circle the frequency adverb that best completes each statement.

1 She (often / hardly ever / never) plays golf.

2 He (often / sometimes / always) goes to the gym four times a week.

3 She (often / sometimes / never) plays tennis in the park.

4 He (always / often / never) goes swimming.

5 She (always / sometimes / never) rides her bike on weekends.

CONVERSATION MODEL

A 🔊 Read and listen to two people talking about habitual activities.

A: Hey, Nancy. Where are you off to?

B: Hi, Trish. I'm going to the gym.

A: Really? Don't you usually go there on weekends?

B: Yes. But not <u>this</u> weekend.

A: How come?

B: Because this weekend I'm going to the beach.

B 🔊 **Rhythm and intonation** Listen again and repeat. Then practice the Conversation Model with a partner.

C Find the grammar Look at the Conversation Model again. Underline one example of the simple present tense and two examples of the present continuous. Which one has future meaning?

NOW YOU CAN   Talk about habitual activities

A Pair work Now change the Conversation Model, using places from the Vocabulary or other places. Then change roles.

A: Hey, ... Where are you off to?

B: Hi, ... I'm going to the ....

A: Really? Don't you usually go there on ....?

B: Yes. But not this ....

A: How come?

B: Because .... I'm ....

Don't stop!
• Ask about the activities your partner does. What do you do at the ___?
• Invite your partner to do something. Why don't we ___ sometime?

B Change partners Practice the conversation again. Use a different place and activity.

BEFORE YOU LISTEN

Warm-up In your opinion, is it important for people to stay in shape? Why? What do people have to do to stay in shape?

LISTENING COMPREHENSION

A 🔊 3:35 **Listen for main ideas** Listen to people talking about their fitness and eating habits. Check the box if the person exercises regularly.

☐ **Jessica Miller**

☐ **Juan Reyneri**

☐ **Naomi Sato**

B 🔊 3:36 **Listen for details** Now listen again and circle the words that complete the statements.

Jessica Miller (walks / runs / swims) to stay in shape. She tries to avoid (fatty / salty / spicy) foods. She likes desserts, but she avoids (candy / chocolate / cookies). She always drinks a lot of (soda / juice / water).

To stay in shape, Juan Reyneri goes running and (does aerobics / lifts weights / goes swimming). He eats five or six (small / medium / large) meals each day. He usually avoids sodas and (chips / sweets / fries). He (often / occasionally / never) eats junk food.

Naomi Sato sometimes goes (walking / running / swimming). She doesn't have much time to (cook / exercise / eat). She eats (fish / meat / vegetables) once a week and lots of (soup / candy / salads).

C Discussion

1 Which of the people above do you think are in shape or out of shape? Explain.

2 Whose fitness and eating habits are like your own? Explain.

PRONUNCIATION *Third-person singular –s: Review*

A 🔊 3:37 Read and listen to the three third-person singular endings. Then listen again and repeat.

/s/	/z/	/ɪz/
sleeps	goes	watches
eats	plays	exercises
works	avoids	munches

B Pair work Take turns reading the statements in Exercise B. Listen for details, practicing third-person singular endings.

A Frame your ideas Take the health survey.

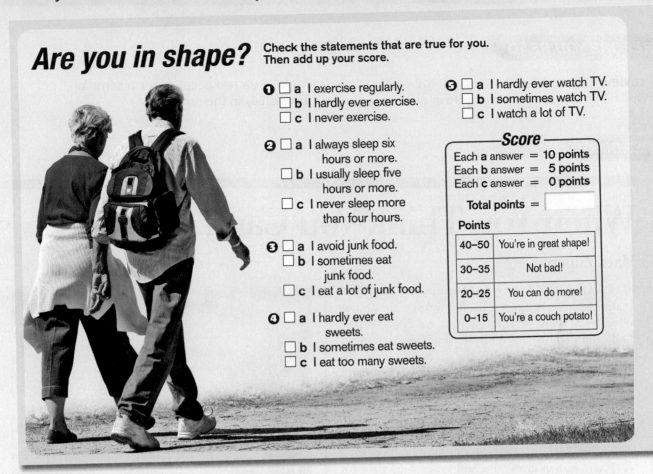

Are you in shape? Check the statements that are true for you. Then add up your score.

1
- ☐ **a** I exercise regularly.
- ☐ **b** I hardly ever exercise.
- ☐ **c** I never exercise.

2
- ☐ **a** I always sleep six hours or more.
- ☐ **b** I usually sleep five hours or more.
- ☐ **c** I never sleep more than four hours.

3
- ☐ **a** I avoid junk food.
- ☐ **b** I sometimes eat junk food.
- ☐ **c** I eat a lot of junk food.

4
- ☐ **a** I hardly ever eat sweets.
- ☐ **b** I sometimes eat sweets.
- ☐ **c** I eat too many sweets.

5
- ☐ **a** I hardly ever watch TV.
- ☐ **b** I sometimes watch TV.
- ☐ **c** I watch a lot of TV.

Score

Each **a** answer = 10 points
Each **b** answer = 5 points
Each **c** answer = 0 points

Total points = ☐

Points

40–50	You're in great shape!
30–35	Not bad!
20–25	You can do more!
0–15	You're a couch potato!

B Pair work Compare your answers and scores on the survey.

C Group work Walk around the classroom and ask questions. Write names and take notes on the chart.

Don't stop!
Ask for more information.

Why are you out of shape?
What junk foods do you eat?
Where do you exercise?

Find someone who . . .	Name	Other information
is in great shape.	Dan	goes running every day

Find someone who . . .	Name	Other information
is in great shape.		
is out of shape.		
eats a lot of junk food.		
avoids sweets.		
avoids fatty foods.		
never sleeps more than four hours.		

D Discussion Now discuss fitness and eating habits. Tell your classmates about the people on your chart.

❝Dan is in great shape. He goes running every day.❞

GOAL | **Describe someone's routines**

Preview Look only at the titles, photos, and captions. What do these two people have in common? What do you think they have to do in order to participate successfully in their sports?

READING 🔊 3:38

When You Think You Can't . . .

Mark Zupan

 A terrible accident in 1993 made Mark Zupan a quadriplegic and changed his life forever. He cannot move his arms or legs normally, and he has to take medication so his legs don't shake. However, after a lot of hard work, he can now use his arms to move his wheelchair, and he can even stand for a short time and take a few slow steps. Zupan—or Zup to his friends—plays quad rugby—a sport for people in wheelchairs. He's a quad rugby champion, winning a gold medal in the 2008 Paralympic Games. "I dream about running all the time," he says, "but you can't live in the past."

Today, Zupan gives talks and raises money for his sport. Anyone who spends time with him forgets that he's in a wheelchair. He lifts weights at the gym every day, drives a car, and goes to rock concerts. "A lot of people think quadriplegics can't do anything," he says. To stay in shape, Zupan is careful about his diet and avoids unhealthy and fatty foods. "Just think of me as a human being and an athlete. Because that's who I am."

The 2005 movie *Murderball* made Zupan a star.

Sources: *Gimp,* HarperCollins, 2006 and cnn.com

Bethany Hamilton

 Surfer Bethany Hamilton had a dream. She wanted to be a champion in her sport. But in 2003, she lost her left arm when she was attacked by a shark in Hawaii. Three weeks later, she was surfing again. Because she can only use one arm, she has to use her legs more to help her go in the right direction. She's a strong competitive surfer, winning first place in 2005 in the NSSA National Championships. She appears on TV and writes books about her experience.

Hamilton wants to help other people follow their dreams, even when they face great difficulties. "People can do whatever they want if they just set their hearts to it, and just never give up . . . Just go out there and do it," she says.

Hamilton was attacked by a tiger shark in 2003.

A Infer information Complete the paragraph about Mark Zupan. Use <u>can</u>, <u>can't</u>, or <u>has to</u>.

Zupan .... spend most of his time in a wheelchair, but he .... stand up
        1   2

or take a few steps for a short time. He .... go walking or running, but he
                                                 3

.... play quad rugby. He .... be careful about his diet so he doesn't get out of
 4   5

shape. He doesn't have complete use of his hands, but he .... lift weights.
                                                       6

He .... drive a car using his feet, but he .... use his hands. A lot of people
     7   8

think quadriplegics .... do anything, but Zupan proves that they ....
                    9   10

B Summarize First, complete the paragraph about Hamilton. Use the simple present tense
or the present continuous. Then on a separate sheet of paper, write a similar paragraph,
summarizing Mark Zupan's routines.

When she surfs, Hamilton .... her legs to help her go in the right direction.
                                      1 use

She .... regularly with the world's top woman surfers, and sometimes
          2 compete

she .... In the photo on page 70, she .... next to her
        3 win   4 stand

surfboard, and she .... because she .... again now. Hamilton
                         5 smile   6 surf

.... to help other people with difficult experiences
    7 want

follow their dreams.

> On your *ActiveBook* Self-Study Disc:
> **Extra Reading Comprehension Questions**

NOW YOU CAN   **Describe someone's routines**

A Notepadding Write some notes about your daily routines.

List some things you usually do . . .	List some things you . . .
• in the morning.	• can't do every day. Explain why.
• in the afternoon.	• have to do every day. Explain why.
• in the evening.	• don't have to do every day. Explain why.

B Pair work Interview your partner about his or her daily routines.

C Group work Now describe your partner's daily routines to your classmates.

> ❝ What are some things you usually do in the morning? ❞

> My partner usually gets up at 7:00. But, on Saturdays, she doesn't have to get up early.

A 3:39 🔊 **Listening comprehension** Listen to the conversations.
Check the statements that are true.

1 ☐ He doesn't exercise regularly.
  ☐ He avoids junk food.
  ☐ He never watches TV.

2 ☐ She's in great shape.
  ☐ She hardly ever goes swimming.
  ☐ She exercises regularly.

3 ☐ He exercises regularly.
  ☐ He has to be careful about calories.
  ☐ He can eat everything he wants.

4 ☐ Heeley can't use his legs.
  ☐ Heeley can't see.
  ☐ Heeley doesn't need help.

B What activities can you do in these places? Write sentences with <u>can</u>.

an athletic field	I can play . . .
a gym	
a park	

C Choose the best response.

1 "Why don't we go swimming tomorrow?"
  a Well, have a great time.   **b** Sorry, I can't. I have to work.

2 "Why don't we meet at 8:00?"
  a Great! When's good for you?   **b** Sure. Sounds great.

3 "What are you up to?"
  a I can't. I have to meet my sister.   **b** I'm having dinner.

D Answer the questions with real information. Use the simple present
tense or the present continuous in your answer.

1 How often do you go to English class?
  (YOU) ....

2 What do you usually do on weekends?
  (YOU) ....

3 What are you doing this weekend?
  (YOU) ....

3:40/3:41
🎵 **Top Notch Pop**
"A Typical Day"
Lyrics p. 150

E **Writing** On a separate sheet of paper, write an interview in which
someone asks you about your exercise and health habits.

Q: What do you do to stay in shape?
A: Well, I run every morning and I lift weights.
Q: Where do you usually . . . ?

WRITING BOOSTER ▸ p. 145

• *Punctuation of statements
  and questions*
• *Guidance for Exercise E*

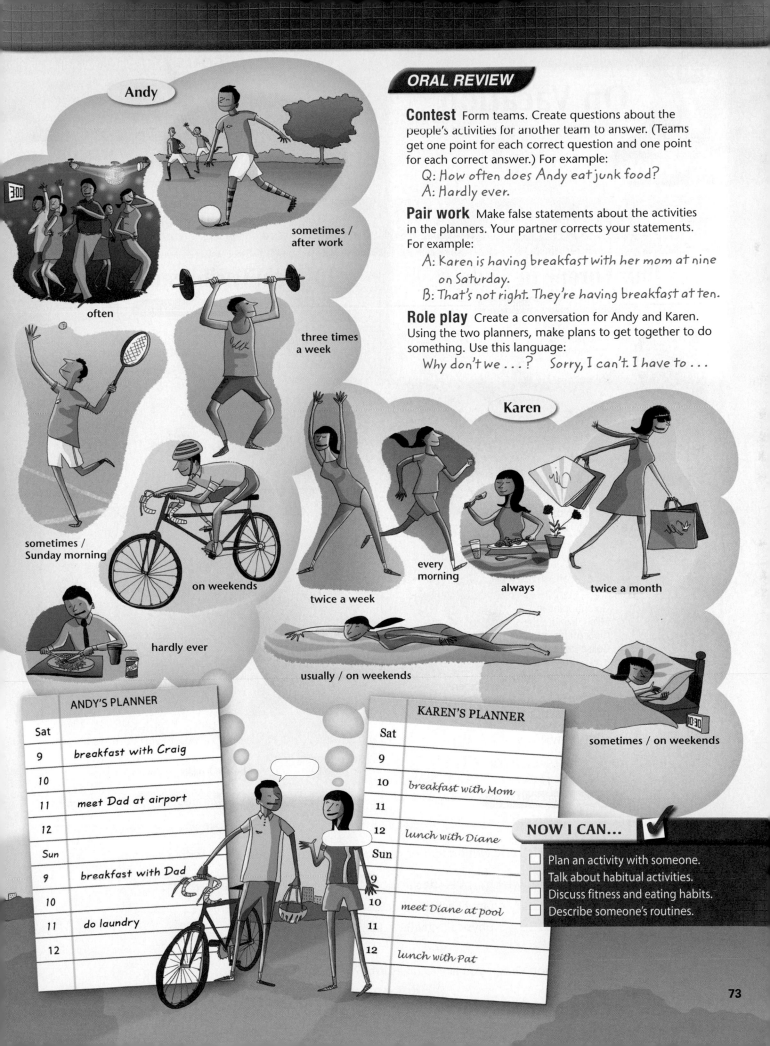

Andy

sometimes / after work

often

three times a week

sometimes / Sunday morning

on weekends

twice a week

every morning

always

twice a month

hardly ever

usually / on weekends

Karen

sometimes / on weekends

ORAL REVIEW

Contest Form teams. Create questions about the people's activities for another team to answer. (Teams get one point for each correct question and one point for each correct answer.) For example:

Q: How often does Andy eat junk food?
A: Hardly ever.

Pair work Make false statements about the activities in the planners. Your partner corrects your statements. For example:

A: Karen is having breakfast with her mom at nine on Saturday.
B: That's not right. They're having breakfast at ten.

Role play Create a conversation for Andy and Karen. Using the two planners, make plans to get together to do something. Use this language:

Why don't we . . . ?   Sorry, I can't. I have to . . .

ANDY'S PLANNER

Sat	
9	breakfast with Craig
10	
11	meet Dad at airport
12	
Sun	
9	breakfast with Dad
10	
11	do laundry
12	

KAREN'S PLANNER

Sat	
9	
10	breakfast with Mom
11	
12	lunch with Diane
Sun	
9	
10	meet Diane at pool
11	
12	lunch with Pat

NOW I CAN...

- [ ] Plan an activity with someone.
- [ ] Talk about habitual activities.
- [ ] Discuss fitness and eating habits.
- [ ] Describe someone's routines.

On Vacation

GOALS After Unit 7, you will be able to:

1 Greet someone arriving from a trip.
2 Ask about someone's vacation.
3 Discuss vacation preferences.
4 Describe good and bad travel experiences

TRAVEL SPECIALS *Guaranteed!* Your money refunded if your flight or cruise is canceled.

Tour Europe in 10 days

Fly to London on July 15.

Take pictures at London's Buckingham Palace.

Visit the Eiffel Tower in Paris and ride a boat on the Seine.

Go shopping in Milan. Explore the ruins of the Coliseum in Rome.

Enjoy Vienna's famous desserts. Walk along the old Berlin Wall.

See Copenhagen's Little Mermaid statue.

Fly back home on July 25.

10-night Caribbean Cruise

Leave from Miami on July 15.

Swim in our heated pool ... or just lie in the sun all day. Eat in our excellent restaurants. And at night, watch a movie or a show ... or go dancing!

Go windsurfing in Montego Bay.

Go snorkeling in Cozumel. Explore a beautiful beach in Costa Rica.

Return to Miami on July 25.

A Pair work Complete the chart by writing <u>tour</u> or <u>cruise</u>. Then discuss your answers with a partner.

In your opinion, which travel special would be good for someone who likes . . .		
history? _____	family activities? _____	entertainment? _____
culture? _____	physical activities? _____	good food? _____

B Discussion Which vacation would you like to take? Why?

C 🔊 **Photo story** Read and listen to a phone call from someone returning from a trip.

Cindy: Hi, Rick. I'm home!
Rick: Cindy! When did you get back?
Cindy: Just yesterday.
Rick: And did you have a good time?
Cindy: I just loved it. I really needed a vacation!

Rick: So, tell me all about your cruise!
Cindy: Well, the people were really great. The food was incredible. And the weather was perfect.
Rick: And what did you do all day?
Cindy: Plenty. In Montego Bay, I went windsurfing. And I had a lot of fun snorkeling in Cozumel.
Rick: Cool!

Cindy: But most of the time I just enjoyed the sun and did absolutely nothing!
Rick: Now that's my kind of vacation!
Cindy: I can't wait for the next one.
Rick: Well, welcome home.

D **Focus on language** Look at the underlined words and expressions in the Photo Story.

1 Find an expression that means "come home."
....

2 Find three words that mean "very good."
....
....
....

E **Think and explain** Complete the statements.

1 When Rick says, "Now that's my kind of vacation!" he means ....
....

2 When Cindy says, "I can't wait for the next one," she means ....
....

F **Discussion** Which part of Cindy's vacation is "your kind of vacation"?

G **Pair work** Complete the questionnaire. Then tell your partner what you usually do on your vacations. Ask about your partner's vacations.

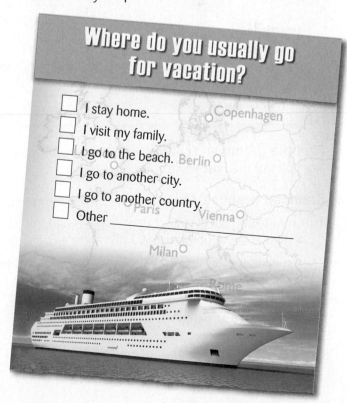

Where do you usually go for vacation?

- ☐ I stay home.
- ☐ I visit my family.
- ☐ I go to the beach.
- ☐ I go to another city.
- ☐ I go to another country.
- ☐ Other _____

GOAL Greet someone arriving from a trip

CONVERSATION MODEL

A 🔊)) **4:03** Read and listen to someone greeting a person arriving from a trip.

A: Welcome back!

B: Thanks.

A: So, how was the flight?

B: Pretty nice, actually.

A: That's good. Can I give you a hand?

B: That's OK. I'm fine.

A: Are you sure?

B: Absolutely. Thanks!

B 🔊)) **4:04** **Rhythm and intonation** Listen again and repeat. Then practice the Conversation Model with a partner.

GRAMMAR   *The past tense of <u>be</u>: Review*

| I He She It | was wasn't | on time. | We You They | were weren't | late. |

Contractions
wasn't = was not
weren't = were not

Questions

Was your flight long? (Yes, it was. / No, it wasn't.)
Were your friends with you? (Yes, they were. / No, they weren't.)

How **was** the traffic? (It was terrible.)
How long **were** you away? (Two weeks.)

GRAMMAR BOOSTER ▸ p. 134

• *The past tense of <u>be</u>: form*

A **Find the grammar** Look at the Photo Story on page 75. Find three examples of the past tense of <u>be</u>.

B **Grammar practice** Complete the conversations with the affirmative or negative past tense of <u>be</u>.

1 **A:** Welcome back! How .... the drive?
   B: Not great. The traffic .... really awful.
      There .... so many cars on the road!
   A: Too bad. .... you alone?
   B: No. My brother .... with me.

2 **A:** Did you just get in?
   B: Yes. My flight .... a little late.
   A: .... there a lot of people on the plane?
   B: No, there ....

3 **A:** Where .... you last week?
   B: We .... on a cruise.
   A: Really? How .... it?
   B: It .... pretty short. Only three days!

4 **A:** So, how .... your parents' trip?
   B: Actually, it .... too great.
   A: What happened?
   B: Their train .... four hours late,
      so they .... really tired.

Adjectives to describe trips

A 🔊 4:05 Read and listen. Then listen again and repeat.

It was so **comfortable**.

It was quite **scenic**.

It was really **boring**.

It was kind of **bumpy**.

It was pretty **scary**.

FLIGHT TIME 1 HOUR   FLIGHT TIME 13 HOURS

It was rather **short**. / It was very **long**.

Intensifiers
so
pretty
really
quite
very
kind of
rather

B Pair work Use the adjectives and intensifiers in the Vocabulary to describe a trip you took.

> ❝ Last year, I went to a small town in the mountains. The bus trip was very bumpy. ❞

Types of trips
a flight   a [bus / train] trip
a drive   a cruise

NOW YOU CAN | Greet someone arriving from a trip

A Pair work Greet someone arriving from a trip. Change the Conversation Model, using the adjectives and intensifiers and the past tense of <u>be</u>. Then change roles.

A: Welcome back!

B: ....

A: So, how was the ....?

B: ...., actually.

A: That's .... Can I give you a hand?

B: ....

> **Don't stop!** Ask your partner other questions about the trip:
> Were there a lot of people on the ___ ?
> How long was the ___ ?

Responses

comfortable
scenic } **That's good!**
short

boring
bumpy
scary } **That's too bad!**
long

B Change partners Greet someone arriving from another type of trip. Use other adjectives from the Vocabulary. Ask more questions.

GOAL Ask about someone's vacation

GRAMMAR BOOSTER ▸ p. 135

GRAMMAR *The simple past tense: Review*

I She It They	**arrived** at three. **didn't arrive** until six.

Did he **have** a good time? (Yes, he did.)
Did they **cancel** your flight? (No, they didn't.)

Where **did** you **go**? (We went to Italy.)
When **did** they **get back**? (On Tuesday.)
What **did** she **do** every day? (She visited museums.)
How many countries **did** you **see**? (Three.)

Regular verbs: spelling

+ <u>ed</u>	+ <u>d</u>	+ <u>ied</u>
visit**ed**	arriv**ed**	study → stud**ied**
watch**ed**	chang**ed**	try → tr**ied**
play**ed**	lik**ed**	

4:06
🔊 **Some irregular verbs**

buy	**bought**	find	**found**	leave	**left**	sleep	**slept**
come	**came**	fly	**flew**	lose	**lost**	spend	**spent**
do	**did**	get	**got**	meet	**met**	steal	**stole**
drink	**drank**	go	**went**	ride	**rode**	swim	**swam**
eat	**ate**	have	**had**	see	**saw**	take	**took**

See page 122 for a more complete list.

• *The simple past tense: more on spelling, usage, and form*

A Find the grammar Look at the Photo Story on page 75.
Circle all the verbs in the simple past tense. Which are irregular verbs?

B Grammar practice Complete Joan's postcard with past forms of the verbs.

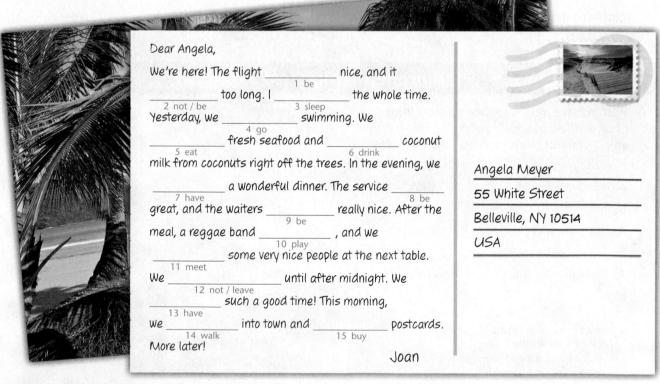

Dear Angela,

We're here! The flight _____ nice, and it
      1 be
_____ too long. I _____ the whole time.
2 not / be   3 sleep
Yesterday, we _____ swimming. We
     4 go
_____ fresh seafood and _____ coconut
5 eat   6 drink
milk from coconuts right off the trees. In the evening, we
_____ a wonderful dinner. The service _____
7 have   8 be
great, and the waiters _____ really nice. After the
     9 be
meal, a reggae band _____ , and we
     10 play
_____ some very nice people at the next table.
11 meet
We _____ until after midnight. We
   12 not / leave
_____ such a good time! This morning,
13 have
we _____ into town and _____ postcards.
  14 walk   15 buy
More later!

                Joan

Angela Meyer

55 White Street

Belleville, NY 10514

USA

C Pair work Write five questions about Joan's vacation, using the simple past tense.
Then practice asking and answering your questions with a partner.

Example:

What did she do on the flight?   2 ....   4 ....

1 ....   3 ....   5 ....

D Grammar practice Imagine that you just got back from one of the vacations on page 74. On a separate sheet of paper, write at least five sentences describing what you did, using the simple past tense.

We left Miami on July 15. . . .

PRONUNCIATION   *The simple past tense ending: Regular verbs*

4:07

🔊))) Listen to the pronunciation of the simple past tense ending –ed. Then listen again and repeat. Practice saying each word on your own.

/d/	/t/	/ɪd/
played	watched	visited
rained	cooked	needed
called	stopped	waited

Be careful!
rained = /reɪnd/   NOT   /reɪnɪd/
watched = /watʃt/   NOT   /watʃɪd/

CONVERSATION MODEL

4:08

A 🔊))) Read and listen to someone describing a vacation.

A: Were you on vacation?

B: Yes, I was. I went to Paris.

A: No kidding! Did you have a good time?

B: Fantastic. I stayed in a really nice hotel and ate at some wonderful restaurants.

A: That sounds nice. Tell me more.

4:09

B 🔊))) **Rhythm and intonation** Listen again and repeat. Then practice the Conversation Model with a partner.

PERTH, AUSTRALIA
GO SURFING
PLAY ON THE BEACH ALL DAY

NOW YOU CAN   Ask about someone's vacation

A Pair work Change the Conversation Model, using the vacation ads and positive adjectives. Then change roles.

A: Were you on vacation?

B: Yes, I was. I ....

A: ....! Did you have a good time?

B: .... I .... and ....

A: That sounds .... Tell me more.

Positive adjectives
incredible   terrific
fantastic   wonderful
great   perfect

COME TO EGYPT
RIDE A CAMEL
VISIT THE GREAT PYRAMIDS

Don't stop! Ask and answer more questions, using the simple past tense.
Did you ___ ?   Where ___ ?
What ___ ?   When ___ ?

BUENOS AIRES,
ARGENTINA!
EAT A DELICIOUS STEAK
DANCE THE TANGO

VISIT NEW YORK!
GO SHOPPING
SEE A BROADWAY PLAY

B Change partners Practice the conversation again about a different vacation.

BEFORE YOU READ

A 🔊 4:10 **Vocabulary** • *Adjectives for vacations* Read and listen. Then listen again and repeat.

Also remember:
boring   fantastic
cool   scenic

It was **relaxing**.   It was **exciting**.   It was **interesting**.   It was **unusual**.

B Pair work Use the Vocabulary to describe one of your vacations.

" Last year, I went to the beach. It was so relaxing. "

READING 🔊 4:11

World Traveler *Did you have a good time?*

Our readers share their experiences on our most popular vacation packages.

ADVENTURE IN CHILE

Go skiing and snowboarding in Valle Nevado

Just 60 kilometers / 37 miles from Santiago

"We just got back! There was nothing but sun and snow, but there was plenty to do. We went dancing every night in a terrific disco. We swam every day in a heated pool and worked out in an incredible gym. The shopping was terrific! And there were so many great restaurants to choose from. Oh, and I almost forgot . . . the views of the Andes Mountains were amazing!"

—Alison Nack, Montreal, Canada

TAKE IT EASY IN THAILAND

Enjoy some of the world's top spas

Luxury and service at prices you can afford

"Back home, we work very hard, and we really needed a vacation. The staff at the spa knew just how to take care of us. My wife and I got wonderful massages and other spa treatments. They even put hot rocks on our backs! We enjoyed excellent healthy meals every day. We loved our spa vacation in Thailand. It was really hard to come back home!"

—Kenji Watanabe, Nagoya, Japan

Global Village Project

Learn about another culture and help the world

No experience necessary

"My vacation in Tajikistan lasted twenty-six days, and we helped to build new homes for ten of those days. The other days we went sightseeing and bought souvenirs. The people were incredibly nice, and I loved the food. There were twelve other volunteers on this trip. The work was actually fun, and we got to know each other really well. In the end we felt really good. I'd definitely do it again!"

—Arturo Manuel Reyes, Monterrey, Mexico

Sources: skitotal.com; spastay.com; habitat.org

A Activate language from a text Find the expressions below in the Reading. Then use them to talk about a vacation you took.

- "There was plenty to do."
- "It was really hard to come back home."
- "I'd definitely do it again."

> 66 In 2004 I went on a cruise. There was plenty to do. I went swimming and 99

B Draw conclusions Choose a vacation package from page 80 for each person. Explain your reasons.

> 66 I love to meet new people and learn how to do new things. 99

> 66 I love sports. I always like to do something new and exciting. 99

> 66 I like to go to places where other people don't go—off the beaten path. 99

> 66 I need a vacation where I don't have to do anything. 99

C Identify supporting details Now choose one of the vacations for yourself. Explain why you chose it. Use the Vocabulary on page 80.

On your *ActiveBook* Self-Study Disc:
Extra Reading Comprehension Questions

NOW YOU CAN | **Discuss vacation preferences**

A Frame your ideas Complete the questionnaire. Then compare answers with a partner.

Need a Vacation? Check all your preferences:

How often do you go on vacation? ☐ never ☐ once or twice a year ☐ more than twice a year

I prefer vacations that are . . .
- ☐ relaxing
- ☐ exciting
- ☐ interesting
- ☐ unusual
- ☐ inexpensive
- ☐ scenic
- ☐ other _____

I like vacations with . . .
- ☐ lots of history and culture
- ☐ nature and wildlife
- ☐ sports and physical activities
- ☐ family activities
- ☐ great entertainment
- ☐ people who speak my language
- ☐ top-notch hotels
- ☐ great food
- ☐ warm weather
- ☐ beautiful beaches
- ☐ friendly people
- ☐ other _____
  _____

Do you need a vacation right now? ☐ Not really. ☐ Maybe. ☐ You bet I do!

B Discussion Now discuss your vacation preferences. Tell your classmates what's important to you.

> 66 For me, warm weather and great entertainment are pretty important. 99

GOAL Describe good and bad travel experiences

BEFORE YOU LISTEN

A 🔊 **Vocabulary •** *Bad and good travel experiences* Read and listen. Then listen again and repeat.

4:12

Bad experiences

The weather was { **horrible.**
awful.
pretty bad.
terrible.

The people were { **unfriendly.**
cold.

They lost my luggage.

Someone stole my wallet.

Good experiences

The weather was { **amazing.**
fantastic.
terrific.
wonderful.

The people were { **friendly.**
warm.

They found my luggage.

Someone returned my wallet.

B Look at the pictures. Complete the sentences.

1 .Someone stole. my purse. **2** The food .... **3** The waiters ....

4 The entertainment .... **5** .... my luggage.

A 🔊 4:13 **Listen for main ideas** Listen to the conversations. Check whether, at the end of the vacation, the person had a good experience or a bad one.

1 ☐ a good experience   ☐ a bad experience   3 ☐ a good experience   ☐ a bad experience
2 ☐ a good experience   ☐ a bad experience   4 ☐ a good experience   ☐ a bad experience

B 🔊 4:14 **Listen for details** Listen again and complete the statements about each vacation.

1 The food was really (good / bad).
The room was (great / terrible).
The entertainment was really (good / bad).

2 The hotel was (terrible / terrific).
Someone stole their (luggage / car).
Disney World was (horrible / wonderful).

3 He didn't have any more (clothes / money).
The people were very (nice / cold).
The hotel was (great / terrible).
Someone stole his (passport / laptop).

4 The food was (great / awful).
The people were (cold / nice).
The vacation was too (short / long).

NOW YOU CAN   Describe good and bad travel experiences

A **Notepadding** Make a list of some of your good and bad travel experiences.

Good experiences	Bad experiences
I went to Bangkok, and the people were really friendly.	When I went to Los Angeles, they lost my luggage.

Good experiences	Bad experiences

Ideas
• the trip
• the weather
• the food
• the service
• the hotels
• the people
• the activities
• your luggage

B **Pair work** Now tell your partner about the good and bad travel experiences you listed. Ask questions about your partner's experiences.

♻ **Be sure to recycle this language.**

Ask
How was the ___ ?
What did you ___ ?
When did you ___ ?
How many ___ did you ___ ?
Tell me about ___ .

Respond
That's good.
That's great!
No kidding!
Oh, no!
That's too bad.
I'm sorry to hear that.

Describe
I had a ___ time.
The [flight] was ___ .
The ___ drove me crazy.
The ___ didn't work.
I was in the mood for ___ , but ___ .
They didn't accept credit cards.

Review

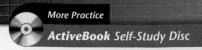
A ◀)) **Listening comprehension** Listen to each person describing a travel experience.
Write the number of the speaker in the box for the type of trip he or she took.

☐ a drive   ☐ a train trip   ☐ a flight   ☐ a beach vacation

B ◀)) Listen again. Circle the adjective that best describes each experience.

1 Her trip was very (short / scary / scenic).

2 His trip was quite (scary / unusual / relaxing).

3 Her trip was pretty (short / scary / boring).

4 His trip was really (short / scenic / boring).

C Complete each conversation with a question in the simple past tense.

1 A: .... on vacation?
   B: We went to Greece.

2 A: .... stay there?
   B: Two weeks.

3 A: .... every day?
   B: We walked along the beach and enjoyed the sun.

4 A: .... get back home?
   B: Last night.

D Complete each statement or question about vacations. Use the past tense form.

1 (we / buy) .... a lot of fantastic things on our vacation.

2 (where / you / eat) .... dinner last night?

3 (we / sleep) .... right on the beach. (it / be) ....
   so relaxing.

4 (my sister / get back) .... last weekend. (she / have)
   .... an amazing time.

5 (my friend / eat) .... some rather good food on her trip to Hong Kong.

6 (when / she / arrive) .... at the hotel?

7 (I / have) .... a terrible time. (the people / be)
   .... quite unfriendly.

8 (we / see) .... an interesting play in London. And (it / be)
   .... pretty inexpensive.

9 (my wife and I / go running) .... every morning
   on the beach during our vacation.

10 (my brother / meet) .... some unusual people on his trip.

E **Writing** On a separate sheet of paper, write about a vacation you took.
Answer these questions.

- Where did you go?
- How was the travel?
- How was the weather?
- What did you do?
- Did you have a good time?

WRITING BOOSTER ▸ p. 145

- Time order
- Guidance for Exercise E

4:17/4:18

♩ **Top Notch Pop**
"My Dream Vacation"
Lyrics p. 150

In 2010, I went on a great trip to . . .

Contest Form two teams. Each team takes turns making a statement about the vacation, using the simple past tense. Continue until one team cannot say anything more. (Each team has thirty seconds to make a statement.)

Role play Create a conversation for the two women on February 5. Start like this:

Were you on vacation?

Pair work Choose one of the vacation pictures. Create a conversation. Start with one of these, or your own idea:

- Can I give you a hand?
- This bed is terrible!
- Excuse me!
- This is so relaxing.

January 15

ARRIVALS

January 17-22

February 5

NOW I CAN... ✓

- [ ] Greet someone arriving from a trip.
- [ ] Ask about someone's vacation.
- [ ] Discuss vacation preferences.
- [ ] Describe good and bad travel experiences.

Shopping for Clothes

GOALS After Unit 8, you will be able to

1 Shop and pay for clothes.
2 Ask for a different size or color.
3 Navigate a mall or department store.
4 Discuss clothing do's and don'ts.

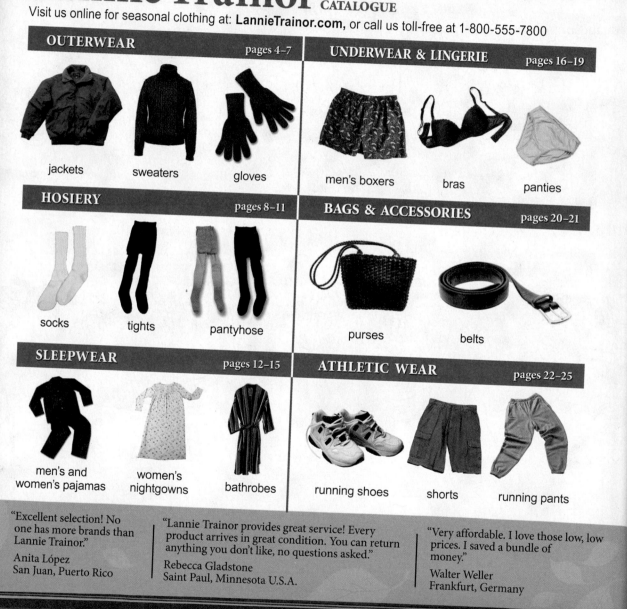

Lannie Trainor CATALOGUE

Visit us online for seasonal clothing at: **LannieTrainor.com,** or call us toll-free at 1-800-555-7800

OUTERWEAR   pages 4–7

jackets   sweaters   gloves

HOSIERY   pages 8–11

socks   tights   pantyhose

SLEEPWEAR   pages 12–15

men's and
women's pajamas   women's
nightgowns   bathrobes

UNDERWEAR & LINGERIE   pages 16–19

men's boxers   bras   panties

BAGS & ACCESSORIES   pages 20–21

purses   belts

ATHLETIC WEAR   pages 22–25

running shoes   shorts   running pants

"Excellent selection! No one has more brands than Lannie Trainor."

Anita López
San Juan, Puerto Rico

"Lannie Trainor provides great service! Every product arrives in great condition. You can return anything you don't like, no questions asked."

Rebecca Gladstone
Saint Paul, Minnesota U.S.A.

"Very affordable. I love those low, low prices. I saved a bundle of money."

Walter Weller
Frankfurt, Germany

A 4:19 🔊 **Vocabulary** • *Clothing departments* Listen and repeat.

B Discussion What clothes are good to buy from a catalogue? What do you like to buy from a store? Why?

❝I like to buy running shoes from a store because I want to be sure the size is right.❞

C 🔊 4:20 **Photo story** Read and listen to a conversation between a clerk and a customer about a sweater the customer wants to buy.

Shopper: Excuse me. How much is that V-neck?

Clerk: This red one? It's $55.

Shopper: That's not too bad. And it's really nice.

Shopper: Could I get it in a larger size?

Clerk: Here you go. This one's a medium. Would you like to try it on?

Shopper: No, thanks. I'll just take it. It's a present for my sister. Would you be nice enough to gift wrap it for me?

Clerk: Of course!

Shopper: Chinese speaker; Clerk: Russian speaker

D **Think and explain** Complete each statement. Then explain your answer.

1 The shopper wants to know the ...... of the sweater.

   a price   **b** size

How do you know? She says, " *How much is that V-neck?* .... "

2 She asks the clerk for ....

   a another color   **b** another size

How do you know? The shopper says,

" .... "

3 The clerk brings the shopper a ....

   a different size   **b** different color

How do you know? The clerk says,

" .... "

4 The sweater is ....

   a for the shopper   **b** for a different person

How do you know? The shopper says,

" .... "

E **Focus on language** Complete each statement with a quotation from the Photo Story.

1 The shopper says, " .... " to get the clerk's attention.

2 The shopper says, " .... " to say that the price of the sweater is OK.

3 The clerk says, " .... " when she gives the shopper the second sweater.

F **Personalize** What's important to you when you shop for clothes? Complete the chart.

	← Not important	Important	Very important →
Prices	○	○	○
Brands	○	○	○
Selection	○	○	○
Service	○	○	○

G **Discussion** Compare charts with your classmates. Explain your reasons.

GOAL **Shop and pay for clothes**

VOCABULARY *Types of clothing and shoes*

4:21
🔊 Read and listen. Then listen again and repeat.

casual clothes

sweaters and jackets

shoes

① jeans ② a T-shirt
③ a sweatshirt ④ a polo shirt
⑤ sweatpants

① a crewneck ② a cardigan
③ a turtleneck ④ a V-neck
⑤ a windbreaker ⑥ a blazer

① oxfords ② loafers
③ sandals ④ running shoes
⑤ pumps ⑥ flats

GRAMMAR *Uses of object pronouns*

Subject pronouns		Object pronouns
I	→	me
you	→	you
he	→	him
she	→	her
it	→	it
we	→	us
they	→	them

As direct objects

direct object (noun)
I want **the cardigan**. → direct object (pronoun)
I love **these pumps**. → I want **it**.
I love **them**.

In prepositional phrases

prepositional phrase (with nouns)
We gave the V-neck **to Jane**. → prepositional phrase (with pronouns)
He's buying a blazer **for his wife**. → We gave the V-neck **to her**.
He's buying a blazer **for her**.

In a sentence with both a direct object and a prepositional phrase, the direct object comes first.

We gave **the hat to Jane**. NOT We gave <s>to Jane the hat</s>.
He's buying **it for her**. NOT He's buying <s>for her it</s>.

GRAMMAR BOOSTER ▸ p. 136

• *Direct and indirect objects: usage*

A Grammar practice First, underline the direct object in each sentence. Then complete each conversation, replacing the direct object noun or noun phrase with an object pronoun.

1 A: Did you buy <u>the green sweatpants</u>?
B: Yes, I bought *them* .

2 A: Don't you love these cool windbreakers?
B: Yes, I really love ....

3 A: Should I buy this crewneck over here?
B: No, don't buy ....

4 A: Did you see the blue polo shirts?
B: Yes, I saw .... on that rack.

5 A: Does your daughter want this cardigan?
B: Yes, she wants ....

6 A: Who did she give the old jacket to?
B: She gave .... to me.

B Grammar practice Unscramble the words and phrases to write statements.

1 I / it / for her / am buying ....

2 they / them / for us / are getting ....

3 please / it / to me / give ....

4 for my son-in-law / I / them / need ....

5 it / he / is / finding / for me ....

CONVERSATION MODEL

A 🔊 4:22 Read and listen to a conversation in which someone is paying for clothes.

A: I'll take these polo shirts, please.

B: Certainly. How would you like to pay for them?

A: Excuse me?

B: Cash or charge?

A: Charge, please. And could you gift wrap them for me?

B: Absolutely.

B 🔊 4:23 **Rhythm and intonation** Listen again and repeat. Then practice the Conversation Model with a partner.

C **Find the grammar** Find and circle all the object pronouns in the Conversation Model.

NOW YOU CAN Shop and pay for clothes

A Look at the Vocabulary on page 88, and look back at the clothing catalogue on page 86. Choose three items of clothing you'd like to buy for yourself or as gifts.

B **Pair work** Change the Conversation Model to buy one of the things you chose. Use the correct object pronouns. Then change roles.

A: I'll take ...., please.

B: .... How would you like to pay for ....?

A: Excuse me?

B: Cash or charge?

A: ...., please. And could you gift wrap .... for me?

B: ....

> **Don't stop!**
> Before you pay, ask about other clothing.

C **Change partners** Create another conversation. Use different articles of clothing.

GOAL Ask for a different size or color

VOCABULARY *Clothing that comes in "pairs"*

A 🔊 [4:24] Read and listen. Then listen again and repeat.

(a pair of)
gloves

(a pair of)
pantyhose

(a pair of)
tights

(a pair of)
panties

(a pair of)
pajamas

(a pair of)
shorts

(a pair of)
pants

(a pair of)
boxers

(a pair of)
briefs

(a pair of)
socks

B 🔊 [4:25] **Listening comprehension** Listen to the conversations. Infer the department each shopper should go to.

1 She should go to ....

2 She should go to ....

3 She got them in ....

4 They're in ....

Departments
Men's underwear
Athletic wear
Outerwear
Lingerie
Sleepwear
Hosiery

GRAMMAR *Comparative adjectives*

Use comparative adjectives to compare two people, places, things, or ideas.
Do you have these pants in a **larger** size? This pair is a little tight.
I need shoes that are **more comfortable**. These are very small.
Do you have a pair of **less expensive** gloves? These are just too expensive.

Use <u>than</u> after the adjective when you compare two items.
That suit is **nicer than** the one I'm wearing.
These gloves are **more expensive than** the other ones.

+ **er**	+ **r**	+ **ier**	consonant + **er**	Irregular forms
small → smaller	large → larger	heavy → heav**ier**	big → big**g**er	good → better
cheap → cheap**er**	loose → looser	pretty → prett**ier**	hot → hot**t**er	bad → worse

BUT use <u>more</u> or <u>less</u> with adjectives that have two or more syllables and don't end in –y.
more expensive / **less** comfortable

GRAMMAR BOOSTER ▸ p. 137

• *Comparative adjectives: spelling rules*

A **Grammar practice** Write the opposite of each comparative adjective.

1 smaller ...larger.... 3 lighter .... 5 more expensive ....
2 taller .... 4 tighter .... 6 less popular ....

B Complete each conversation with comparative adjectives. Use <u>than</u> if necessary.

1 A: I just love these pajamas, but I wish they were ....
   warm
   B: What about these? Blue is a really flattering color for you, and they're much ....
   expensive

2 A: Don't take that nightgown to Hawaii! It's .... it is here. Take something ....
   hot   light
   B: Good idea.

3 A: What do you think of these red gloves?
   B: Beautiful. They're .... the black ones. And they're ...., too.
   pretty   cheap

4 A: Excuse me. Do these pants come in a .... length?
   long
   B: I'm sure they do. Let me see if I can find you something ....
   good

CONVERSATION MODEL

A 🔊 4:26 Read and listen to someone asking for a different size.

A: Excuse me. Do you have these gloves in a smaller size? I need a medium.

B: Yes, we do. Here you go.

A: Thanks.

B: Would you like to take them?

A: Yes, please. Thanks for your help.

B: My pleasure.

Sizes
S   small
M   medium
L   large
XL   extra large
XXL   extra extra large

B 🔊 4:27 **Rhythm and intonation** Listen again and repeat. Then practice the Conversation Model with a partner.

NOW YOU CAN   Ask for a different size or color

A **Notepadding** On the notepad, make a list of clothes you'd like to buy.

I'd like to buy:

B **Pair work** Change the Conversation Model. Use comparatives and your list of clothes. Ask for a different size or color. Then change roles.

A: Excuse me. Do you have .... in ....?

B: Yes, we do. Here you go.

A: Thanks.

B: Would you like to take ....?

A: .... Thanks for your help.

B: ....

Don't stop!
• Ask to see other clothes.
• Pay for the clothes.

Ideas
in a smaller size
in a larger size
in a darker / lighter color
in [black, white, etc.]
in size [10, 34, etc.]

C **Change partners** Ask about other types of clothes.

BEFORE YOU LISTEN

4:28
🔊 **Vocabulary** • *Interior locations and directions* Read and listen. Then listen again and repeat.

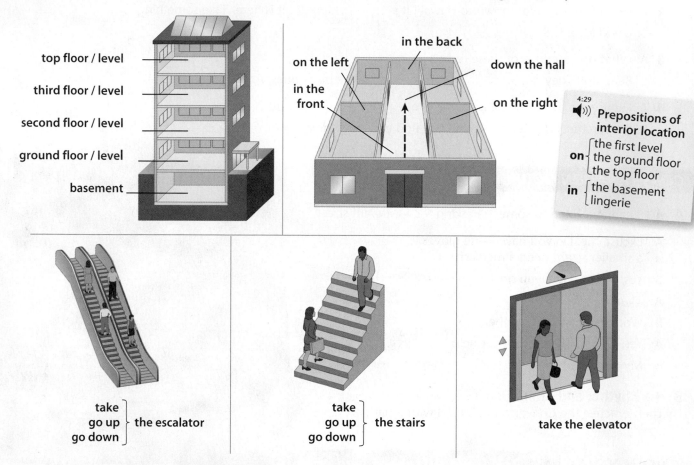

top floor / level

third floor / level

second floor / level

ground floor / level

basement

in the back

on the left

down the hall

in the front

on the right

4:29
🔊 **Prepositions of interior location**

on { the first level, the ground floor, the top floor

in { the basement, lingerie

take / go up / go down } the escalator

take / go up / go down } the stairs

take the elevator

LISTENING COMPREHENSION

4:30
A 🔊 **Understand locations and directions** Listen to directions in a department store. Write the number of each location in the white boxes on the floor diagrams.

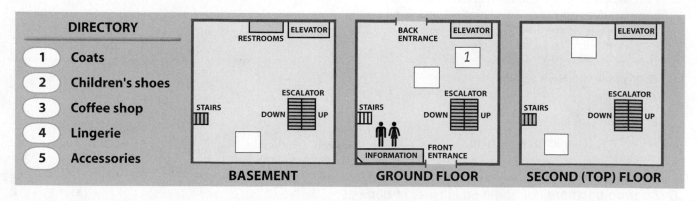

DIRECTORY

1 Coats
2 Children's shoes
3 Coffee shop
4 Lingerie
5 Accessories

RESTROOMS / ELEVATOR / STAIRS / ESCALATOR DOWN UP

BASEMENT

BACK ENTRANCE / ELEVATOR / 1 / STAIRS / ESCALATOR DOWN UP / INFORMATION / FRONT ENTRANCE

GROUND FLOOR

ELEVATOR / STAIRS / ESCALATOR DOWN UP

SECOND (TOP) FLOOR

B Pair work Take turns asking for and giving directions to any of the locations.

A 🔊 4:31 Read and listen. Then listen again and repeat.

A: The shoe department is upstairs, on the third floor.

B: Excuse me? The first floor?

A: No. It's on the third floor.

B Pair work Now practice the conversation with a partner.

NOW YOU CAN Navigate a mall or department store

A Notepadding Choose five departments from the store directory and write one thing you'd like to get in each department.

Department	I'd like . . .
Men's Outerwear	a jacket

Department	I'd like . . .

B Wordposting Put the four categories below on a separate sheet of paper. With a partner, make a list of language you know for each category.

1 Ask for directions
2 Give directions and state locations
3 Ask for a size, color, etc.
4 Pay for things

1	Ask for directions
	I'm looking for the hosiery department.

C Role play Navigate the department store, using the floor plan. Create a conversation between the shopper and the person at the information desk. Use your notepad and your wordposts. Then change partners, roles, and items.

❝ Excuse me. I'm looking for . . . ❞

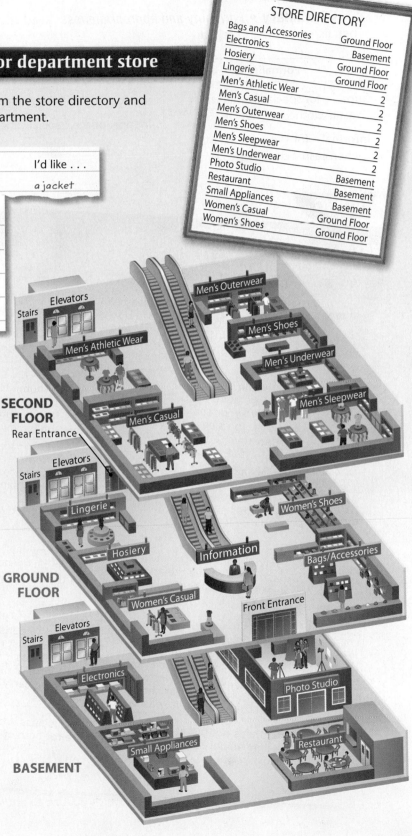

STORE DIRECTORY

Bags and Accessories	Ground Floor
Electronics	Basement
Hosiery	Ground Floor
Lingerie	Ground Floor
Men's Athletic Wear	Ground Floor
Men's Casual	2
Men's Outerwear	2
Men's Shoes	2
Men's Sleepwear	2
Men's Underwear	2
Photo Studio	2
Restaurant	Basement
Small Appliances	Basement
Women's Casual	Basement
Women's Shoes	Ground Floor
	Ground Floor

GOAL Discuss clothing do's and don'ts

 Vocabulary • *Formality and appropriateness* Read and listen to each pair of antonyms. Then listen again and repeat.

Formality	Appropriateness	Strictness
formal for special events when casual clothes are not OK	**appropriate** socially correct	**liberal** without many rules for appropriate dress
informal for everyday events when casual clothes are OK	**inappropriate** socially incorrect	**conservative** with more rules for appropriate dress

READING 4:33

posted by:
Travelin'Girl

Hello! Traveling to Dar es Salaam, Tanzania next week and I need some info on clothing do's and don'ts. I'm in Holland right now where the dress code is pretty liberal, more liberal than where I come from in Germany. The attitude is "anything goes," and they wear some pretty wild things here! How strict are the "rules" there?

posted by:
Jillian25

Hi, Travelin'Girl,
I go there quite a bit, and my general rule of thumb for East Africa is to keep your shoulders covered and to wear below-the-knee pants or skirts—no sleeveless shirts or tank tops. The culture is pretty conservative, and women dress modestly. Don't show too much skin.

posted by:
TallPaul

OK, Jillian25. But it's incredibly hot and humid there, just about all year round. Travelin'Girl should pack for the heat: cotton blouses (in light colors); casual, comfortable, light pants; sandals. She didn't say—is this a business trip or pleasure?

posted by:
Travelin'Girl

A mix of both—a little business in Dar (with my husband), then a quick safari to see the animals. Then I plan on spending at least one weekend at the beach. What's the story there?

posted by:
Jillian25

There really are no hard and fast rules, but in tourist areas like beaches, it's more informal and relaxed, and most modest clothing is OK. A bathing suit's fine at the beach, as long as it's not too revealing. But in general, in towns near the coast, the rules are stricter and it's inappropriate to wear shorts or miniskirts, so carry a piece of cotton cloth that you can fix easily around your waist.

posted by:
TallPaul

And let's not forget your husband. For business and formal meetings, a lightweight suit is always appropriate for both of you (and a tie for him).

Tanzanian woman in modest dress

A Paraphrase Explain in your own words what clothing is appropriate in Tanzania, according to the blog.

B Identify supporting details Check true, false, or no info. Explain the reason why you chose each answer.

	true	false	no info
1 "Jillian25" says she is a travel agent.	☐	☐	☐
2 "Travelin'Girl" wants to dress appropriately in Tanzania.	☐	☐	☐
3 "Travelin'Girl" is traveling alone.	☐	☐	☐
4 Dar is in East Africa.	☐	☐	☐
5 "Travelin'Girl" and her husband have children.	☐	☐	☐
6 Women are expected to dress conservatively in Tanzania.	☐	☐	☐

C Apply information Imagine you are going on the same trip as "Travelin'Girl." Plan your clothes for a one-week visit to Tanzania. Be specific. Explain your choices.

> " I think I'll take three pairs of shorts because this is a vacation and I plan to spend most of my time at the beach . . . "

On your *ActiveBook* Self-Study Disc:
Extra Reading Comprehension Questions

NOW YOU CAN Discuss clothing do's and don'ts

A Frame your ideas Take the opinion survey.

WHAT'S YOUR PERSONAL DRESS CODE?

Check agree or disagree.	agree	disagree
It's OK for men to wear shorts on the street.	☐	☐
It's OK for women to wear shorts on the street.	☐	☐
It's OK to wear sandals in an office.	☐	☐
It's important for men to wear ties in an office.	☐	☐
It's OK for men to wear sleeveless T-shirts in a restaurant.	☐	☐
It's OK for women to wear revealing clothes in a religious institution.	☐	☐

HOW WOULD YOU RATE YOURSELF?

☐   ☐   ☐

CONSERVATIVE   LIBERAL   "ANYTHING GOES!"

B Notepadding With a partner, write some clothing do's and don'ts for visitors to your country. Do the same rules apply to both men and women? Use the survey as a guide.

in offices and formal restaurants:

in casual social settings:

in religious institutions:

C Group work Now discuss clothing do's and don'ts for your country. Does everyone agree?

Text-mining (optional)
Underline language in the Reading on page 94 to use in the Group Work. For example:
"My general rule of thumb is . . ."

Review

A 4:34 🔊 **Listening comprehension** Listen to the conversations. Use the context to infer which department the people are in. Listen more than once if necessary.

1 ....
2 ....
3 ....
4 ....
5 ....

Departments
Shoes
Bags and Accessories
Hosiery
Outerwear
Sleepwear
Lingerie
Electronics

B Complete the chart with the appropriate kinds of shoes and clothes for certain places and occasions.

	Shoes	Clothes
To class or work		
To formal occasions		
On the weekend		

C Complete the travel article with the comparative form of each adjective. Use <u>than</u> when necessary.

When you travel, think carefully about the clothes you pack. As far as color is concerned, ... colsors are usually
1 dark
.... For .... destinations,
2 practical   3 cool
a blazer can be .... a
4 convenient
windbreaker or cardigan because you can wear it in
.... settings such as offices
5 conservative
and .... restaurants. For travel to
6 formal
.... areas of the world, ... clothes are
7 hot   8 light
.... ones.
9 comfortable   10 heavy

4:35/4:36
🎵 **Top Notch Pop**
"Anything Goes"
Lyrics p. 150

D Rewrite each sentence. Change the direct and indirect object nouns and noun phrases to object pronouns.

1 Please show the loafers to my husband. ..... *Please show them to him.* ....

2 They sent the jeans to their grandchildren. ....

3 How is she paying Robert for the clothes? ....

4 When are we buying the gift for Marie? ....

E **Writing** Imagine that you have a friend from another country who is coming to visit you. Write a letter or e-mail to your friend, explaining what to pack for the trip. Give your friend advice on appropriate and inappropriate dress.

WRITING BOOSTER ▸ p. 146

• Connecting ideas with <u>because</u> and <u>since</u>
• Guidance for Exercise E

Hi! Here are some clothing tips for your visit. First
of all, the "rules" here are...

Contest Study the picture. Name all the kinds of sweaters and shoes and kinds of clothing that come in pairs. (The student who can name more kinds wins.)

Pair work With a partner, make comparisons about the clothes. For example:

Blazers are more formal than windbreakers.

Role play Look at the directory. Create conversations for the following people:
• the shoppers and clerks at the information desk
• the customer and the clerk talking about the jackets
• the clerk and the customer paying for clothes

DIRECTORY

BAGS AND ACCESSORIES	1
CHILDREN'S DEPARTMENT	3
ELECTRONICS	3
HAIRDRESSER	4
LINGERIE	1
MEN'S DEPARTMENT	1
PHOTO STUDIO	2
RESTAURANTS	4
SHOES	1
TRAVEL AGENCY	2
WOMEN'S DEPARTMENT	1

NOW I CAN... ✓

☐ Shop and pay for clothes.
☐ Ask for a different size or color.
☐ Navigate a mall or department store.
☐ Discuss clothing do's and don'ts.

97

Taking Transportation

GOALS After Unit 9, you will be able to:

1 Discuss schedules and buy tickets.
2 Book travel services.
3 Understand airport announcements.
4 Describe transportation problems.

Buses from Lima to Nazca

DESTINATION	FREQUENCY	DEPARTURE	ARRIVAL	STOPS	BUS TERMINAL
Lima - Nazca	Daily	04:30	10:45	Paracas	Terminal Nazca
Lima - Nazca	Daily	07:00	13:30	Paracas-Ica	Terminal Nazca
Lima - Nazca	Daily	13:30	20:00	Paracas-Ica	Terminal Nazca
Lima - Nazca	Daily	14:00	20:00	Non-stop	Terminal Nazca
Lima - Nazca	Daily	17:30	23:30	Non-stop	Terminal Nazca

BEIJING to SHANGHAI

Train No.	Depart (BEIJING)	Arrive (SHANGHAI)	Travel Time	Air-conditioned
D31	11:05	20:49	0d 09h 44m	Yes
1461	14:42	12:49	0d 22h 07m	No
Z21	19:32	07:00	0d 11h 28m	Yes
Z13	19:38	07:06	0d 11h 28m	Yes
Z7	19:44	07:12	0d 11h 28m	Yes

CATICLAN to MANILA

Flight No.	Departure	Arrival	Frequency	Aircraft Type
2P 036	0705	0815	DAILY	DH3
2P 038	0725	0835	DAILY	DH3
2P 040	0805	0915	DAILY	DH3
2P 046	1040	1150	DAILY	DH3
2P 048	1700	1810	DAILY	DH3

Sources: mysteryperu.com; travelchinaguide.com; airphils.com

A Use the schedules to find the answers to the questions.

1 It's now 10:00 A.M. When is the next bus to Nazca?

2 And when is the next non-stop bus to Nazca?

3 How much time does it take to get from Beijing to Shanghai on train 1461?

4 Which train is faster, train 1461 or train D31?

5 What time does flight 2P 046 depart for Manila? When does it arrive?

B **Pair work** Ask your partner more questions about each schedule.

C 🔊 **Photo story** Read and listen to a conversation between two people trying to catch a flight.

Marcos: Excuse me. Do you speak English?

Roger: Actually I'm French. But, yes.

Marcos: Thank goodness! I'm looking for Terminal 2.

Roger: No problem. That's where I'm going. Just follow me.

Roger: So where are you flying today?

Marcos: Manila. Then I'm connecting to a flight home.

Roger: Well, that's a coincidence. I'm on my way to Manila, too. Flight 56?

Marcos: Yes. But we should hurry. It's boarding in fifteen minutes.

Roger: And where is home?

Marcos: Brazil. São Paulo.

Roger: No kidding! I'm going to go to São Paulo next week!

Marcos: Really? What a small world!

Marcos: Portuguese speaker; Roger: French speaker

D Focus on language Find an underlined phrase or sentence in the Photo Story that has the same meaning as:

1 I'm traveling to ...   **2** Let's walk faster.   **3** I'm changing to ...

E Think and explain Circle T (<u>true</u>), F (<u>false</u>), or NI (<u>no information</u>). Then explain each answer.

T F NI **1** Flight 56 leaves from Terminal 2.

T F NI **2** Roger lives in France.

T F NI **3** Roger and Marcos are both flying to Manila.

T F NI **4** Marcos is staying in Manila.

T F NI **5** Roger is staying in Manila.

T F NI **6** The two men catch the flight.

F Pair work Complete the chart with the means of transportation you prefer for each occasion. Then discuss your choices with a partner.

To school or work	bus	affordable, convenient, I can read or work.

	Means of transportation	Reason
To school or work		
To social events on weekends		
For vacations in my country		
For vacations outside of my country		

♻️ **Be sure to recycle this language.**

popular	cheap
convenient	scenic
affordable	boring
comfortable	long
expensive	short
relaxing	scary

GOAL Discuss schedules and buy tickets

VOCABULARY *Kinds of tickets and trips*

A 🔊 5:03 Read and listen. Then listen again and repeat.

PASSENGER TICKET
KOREA BUS LINE
SEOUL > SOKCHO

a one-way ticket

PASSENGER TICKET
KOREA BUS LINE
SEOUL > SOKCHO
SOKCHO > SEOUL

a round-trip ticket

JAPAN RAIL	Kodama (local)	Nozomi (express)
Tokyo	10:13	10:20
Odawara	10:30	–
Atami	11:00	–
Maibara	13:39	–
Kyoto	14:04	12:38

the local **the express**

Air China
Flight
009
New York→ Los Angeles→ Taipei

a direct flight

Air China
Flight
808
New York —— Taipei

a non-stop flight

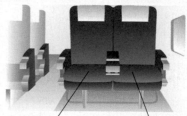

an aisle seat **a window seat**

B Complete the conversations with words and phrases from the Vocabulary.

1 A: Would you like a window or an aisle?

B: .... I like to walk around.

2 A: Is Flight 3 a .... flight?

B: No. It's a .... flight. It makes a stop, but you don't have to change planes.

3 A: Do you want a .... ticket to Rome?

B: Actually, I need a .... I'm not coming back!

4 A: I'm sorry. It's too late to make the ....

B: Well, I'll take .... I'm not in a hurry.

GRAMMAR *Modals should and could*

> **should**
>
> **Use should and the base form of a verb to give advice.**
>
> You **shouldn't take** that flight. You **should take** the non-stop.
> **Should** they **take** the bus? (Yes, they **should**. / No, they **shouldn't**.)
> When **should** we **leave**? (Before 2:00.)
>
> ───
>
> **could**
>
> **Use could and the base form of a verb to suggest or ask about alternatives or possibilities.**
>
> The express bus is full, but you **could take** the local.
> **Could** I **take** the 2:20? (Yes, you **could**. / No, you **couldn't**.)

GRAMMAR BOOSTER ▸ p. 138

• *Modals: form and meaning*
• *Common errors*

A Grammar practice Complete each statement or question with <u>should</u> or <u>could</u> and the base form.

1 .... the express. The local arrives too late.
He / take

2 They said .... two aisle seats or an aisle and a window.
we / have

3 .... a round-trip ticket. That way you won't have to wait in line twice.
   You / get

4 Which train ....? We absolutely have to be there on time.
     we / take

5 .... a ticket at the station or on the train. It doesn't matter.
   They / buy

B **Pair work** Two coworkers are at Penn Station, and they work in Oak Plains. It's 7:20 A.M. They have to arrive in Oak Plains for work at 9:00. Use the schedule to discuss all the possible choices. Use <u>could</u> and <u>should</u>. Explain your choices.

Blue numbers = express trains			
Penn Station	**Northway**	**Oak Plains**	**Carmel**
7:15	7:50	8:30	9:00
7:25	—	8:25	8:55
7:30	—	—	8:55
7:30	8:05	8:45	9:15
7:50	8:25	9:05	9:35

> " They could take the 7:30 express. "

> " No. That train doesn't stop in Oak Plains. "

CONVERSATION MODEL

5:04
A 🔊))) Read and listen to someone buying tickets.

A: Can I still make the 5:12 bus to Montreal?

B: I'm sorry. It left five minutes ago.

A: Too bad. What should I do?

B: Well, you could take the 5:30.

A: OK. One ticket, please.

B: One-way or round-trip?

A: Round-trip, please.

5:05
B 🔊))) **Rhythm and intonation** Listen again and repeat. Then practice the Conversation Model with a partner.

NOW YOU CAN   Discuss schedules and buy tickets

A **Pair work** Use the train departure board. Imagine it is now 7:15. Change the Conversation Model, based on where you want to go. Then change roles.

A: Can I still make the .... train to ....?

B: No, I'm sorry. It left .... minutes ago.

A: .... What should I do?

B: Well, you could take the ....

A: OK. One ticket, please.

B: One-way or round-trip?

A: ...., please.

Don't stop!
• Discuss the price of tickets.
• Ask whether the train makes stops.
• Ask for the kind of seat you'd like.

DEPARTURES	07:15 AM	
TO	DEPARTS	TRACK
OSAKA	06:55	6
NARITA	07:03	9
KYOTO	07:12	19
OSAKA	08:23	8
NARITA	08:26	9
KYOTO	08:31	18

B **Change partners** Practice the conversation again. Discuss other departures.

GOAL **Book travel services**

GRAMMAR *Be going to to express the future: Review*

base form
I'm going to **rent** a car in New York.
She's going to **eat** at the airport.
We're going to **take** a taxi into town.

Remember: The present continuous is also often used to express future plans.
I'm renting a car in New York **next week**.

Are they **going to need** a taxi? (Yes, they are. / No, they aren't.)
Is Beth **going to make** a reservation? (Yes, she is. / No, she isn't.)

When **are** you **going to arrive**? (At noon.)   Who **are** they **going to meet**? (The travel agent.)
Where **is** he **going to wait**? (In the lobby.)   Who's **going to take** me to the airport? (Tom is.)

GRAMMAR BOOSTER ▸ p. 138
• *Expansion: future actions*

A Grammar practice Complete each statement or question with be going to and the base form of the verb.

1 .... tickets for the express.
they / buy

2 When .... for the airport?
she / leave

3 .... an aisle seat?
you / ask for

4 Who .... him to the train station?
take

B Complete the e-mail. Circle the correct verb forms.

Here's my travel information: I (1 leaving / 'm leaving) Mexico City at 4:45 P.M. on Atlas Airlines flight 6702. The flight (2 is arriving / arriving) in Chicago at 9:50 P.M. Mara's flight (3 going to get in / is getting in) ten minutes later, so we (4 're meeting / meeting) at the baggage claim. That's too late for you to pick me up, so I (5 'm going to take / take) a limo from O'Hare. Mara (6 goes to / is going to) come along and (7 spend / spending) the night with us. Her flight to Tokyo (8 not leaving / isn't leaving) until the next day.

C Pair work Ask your partner three questions about his or her future plans. Use be going to.

❝ What are you going to do on your vacation? ❞

VOCABULARY *Travel services*

A 🔊 5:06 Read and listen. Then listen again and repeat.

a rental car

a taxi

a limousine / a limo

a hotel reservation

B 🔊 **Listening comprehension** Listen to the conversations. Then listen again and complete each sentence with <u>be going to</u> and infer the name of a travel service.

1 He .... (reserve) a
.... for her.

2 The tourist .... (need)
a .... in Seoul.

3 She .... (get) a
.... at John F. Kennedy Airport.

4 The agent .... (check) to
see if he can reserve a .... for the tourist.

CONVERSATION MODEL

5:08

A 🔊 Read and listen to a conversation between a travel agent and a traveler.

A: Hello. Baker Travel. Can I help you?

B: I hope so. I'm going to need a car in Dubai.

A: Certainly. What date are you arriving?

B: April 6th.

A: And what time?

B: Let me check . . . 5:45 P.M.

5:09

B 🔊 **Rhythm and intonation** Listen again and repeat. Then practice the Conversation Model with a partner.

C **Find the grammar** Find and circle two ways that A and B express future plans in the Conversation Model.

NOW YOU CAN   Book travel services

A **Pair work** Change the Conversation Model. Book one of the travel services from the Vocabulary. Use the tickets for arrival information. Then change roles.

A: Hello. Can I help you?

B: .... I'm going to need ....
in ....

A: .... What date are you arriving?

B: ....

A: And what time?

B: Let me check . . . .

Don't stop!
Ask for additional services.

❝ I'm also going to need a hotel reservation. ❞

B **Change partners** Make your own flight, bus, or train tickets. Then practice the conversation again, using <u>your</u> tickets.

Your ticket

From _____

To _____

Date _____

Departs _____ Arrives _____

PASSENGER TICKET AND BAGGAGE CHECK

AIR CUZCO   APRIL 11   FLIGHT 22
DEPARTURE: 18:00   ARRIVAL: 19:15

LIMA TO CUZCO

88985376124   0 988 7631986534 7

Seoul Touristbus

FROM   Seoul
TO   Sokcho
DATE   13 August
DEPARTS   07:45
ARRIVES   11:55

BOARDING PASS

EXCELA RAIL TRANSPORT

JUNE 26 EXPRESS TRAIN

NEW YORK TO WASHINGTON

DEPARTURE: 6:00 PM

ARRIVAL: 9:10 PM

BEFORE YOU LISTEN

A 🔊 5:10 **Vocabulary** • *Airline passenger information* Read and listen. Then listen again and repeat.

① **depart**   ② **arrive**   ③ **take off**   ④ **land**   ⑤ **go through security**

Class
ECONOMY CLASS

Flight & Date	Gate	Seat
572	5	27A

Boarding time
From | To | Destination
Bogotá | **Barranquilla**

Name | Airline use
Jane Smith | 0081A | YY227670

Boarding Pass

Some flight problems
- The flight is **overbooked**. The airline sold too many tickets, so some passengers can't board.
- The flight is **delayed**. The flight will depart late.
- The flight is **canceled**. The passengers have to find another flight.

⑥ **the gate**   ⑦ **an agent**
⑧ **a boarding pass**   ⑨ **a passenger**
⑩ **the departure lounge**

B Use the Vocabulary to complete the pre-flight instructions.

When you .... 1 at the airport, you should take your luggage to the check-in counter and get your .... 2 . Then you can .... 3 , where .... 4 have to put all their hand luggage on the belt. From there you should go to the .... 5 your plane is departing from. If you are early and your plane hasn't landed or arrived at the gate, just have a seat in the .... 6 . When your flight is called, you can show your boarding pass to the .... 7 and get on the plane. Be sure to turn off all electronic devices and put on your seat belt before your plane .... 8 from the gate. Enjoy the takeoff, and have a good flight!

LISTENING COMPREHENSION

A 🔊 5:11 **Understand public announcements** Listen to the announcements. Check the travel problems.

- ☐ a delay
- ☐ a gate change
- ☐ a cancellation
- ☐ a security problem
- ☐ an overbooking
- ☐ a mechanical problem

B ◀)) **Listen for details** Listen again and write the flight information.

1 flight number: ....

2 original departure gate: ....

3 final departure gate: ....

4 final departure time: ....

PRONUNCIATION *Intonation for stating alternatives*

5:13

A ◀)) Listen to the rhythm and intonation of alternatives. Then listen again and repeat.

1 Well, you could take the train or the bus.

2 They could wait or reserve a later flight.

3 Would you like one-way or round-trip?

B Now practice saying each sentence on your own.

NOW YOU CAN | **Understand airport announcements**

A Read the announcement by the gate agent for Rapid Air flight 58 from Brasilia to São Paulo. Make sure you understand the details.

> **"** Good afternoon, ladies and gentlemen. Flight 58 is overbooked. We apologize. We need two volunteers to give up their seats on this flight. There are seats available on all later flights to São Paulo. If you volunteer to take a later flight, Rapid Air will give you a free round-trip ticket anywhere we fly. The free ticket is good for one year. **"**

B Pair work Now act on the airport announcement. Imagine that you and your partner have tickets on flight 58. First read the situation:

- The time is now 16:35.
- You have a very important dinner in São Paulo at 20:30.
- The flight takes about two hours gate to gate.

Then look at the departure schedule and discuss your alternatives.

DEPARTURES			
São Paulo	56	16:20	departed
Rio de Janeiro	89	16:40	boarding
São Paulo	58	16:50	now 17:25
São Paulo	60	17:50	on time

We could volunteer. Flight 60 is going to arrive before the dinner. What do you think?

I don't know. I think we should stay on flight 58. There's always a lot of traffic and we'll be late for the dinner.

C Discussion Summarize your decision for the class and explain why you made that decision. How many students decided to take a later flight?

105

GOAL | **Describe transportation problems**

A 🔊 5:14 **Vocabulary** • *Transportation problems* Read and listen. Then listen again and repeat.

We **had an accident**.

We **had mechanical problems**.

We **missed** our **train**.

We **got bumped from** the **flight**.

We **got seasick**.

Also: carsick airsick

B 🔊 5:15 **Listening comprehension** Listen and complete each statement with the Vocabulary.

1 They ....
2 They ....
3 They ....
4 They ....
5 They ....

READING 🔊 5:16

GOT BUMPED FROM A FLIGHT?
Maybe it's not so bad after all...

As most travelers know, airlines commonly overbook flights because of the large and predictable number of "no-shows"—people who have reservations but don't show up for the flight. Overbooking helps airlines limit the number of empty seats on their flights. However, if a flight is overbooked, some passengers with confirmed reservations have to get off the plane.

Getting bumped isn't always a bad thing, however. There is a growing number of passengers who feel lucky if their flight is overbooked. Why? Because airlines have to provide bumped passengers with cash, free flights, hotels, and/or meals to compensate them for their inconvenience.

In fact, airlines usually ask for volunteers to get off an overbooked flight in exchange for those perks, and many passengers say "Sure!" and happily deplane. Some people even make a habit of choosing flights that are likely to be overbooked, just so they can volunteer!

Source: Adapted from airconsumer.ost.gov

Driver blames GPS for train crash

BEDFORD HILLS–Last night, Edward Carter, 43, of White Plains told police that his car's global positioning system (GPS) instructed him to make a wrong turn directly onto the train tracks in Bedford Hills. When he turned, his car became stuck on the track, and he had to abandon the car.

In a statement to the police, the man said he was driving north with his son on the Saw Mill Parkway at about 8 P.M. They planned to go to a restaurant on Route 117.

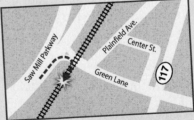
The location of last night's accident

Following the instructions from his GPS unit, he exited the parkway at Green Lane. But then, instead of driving to Route 117 and turning right there, he made a very wrong turn. He turned right at the railroad tracks. The man and his son tried to move the car off the tracks, but they couldn't. Shortly afterward, a Metro-North commuter train hit Mr. Carter's car. Luckily, there were no deaths or injuries. Police say that drivers need to pay attention to the road, not the GPS unit.

Source: Adapted from news articles in lohud.com

Critical thinking Based on the Reading and your own ideas, discuss the following topics.

1 Why do you think people with confirmed reservations become "no-shows"?

2 What are some advantages of getting bumped? Would you volunteer to get off an overbooked flight? Explain.

3 What are some advantages of GPS systems? What are some disadvantages?

4 Do you prefer GPS systems or paper maps? Explain.

On your *ActiveBook* Self-Study Disc:
Extra Reading Comprehension Questions

NOW YOU CAN Describe transportation problems

A Check all the means of transportation you have taken. Then add other means you know.

☐ bus   ☐ train   ☐ taxi   ☐ limousine   ☐ ferry

☐ ship   ☐ airplane   ☐ helicopter   ☐ other ....

B Pair work Ask your partner questions about the means of transportation he or she checked.

> " When was the last time you took a train? "

C Notepadding Choose a time when you had transportation problems. On the notepad, make notes about the trip.

means of transportation:	
month, day, or year of trip:	
destination:	
bad memories:	

D Group work Now tell your story to your classmates. Describe your transportation problems. Ask them questions about their problems.

> You won't believe what happened on my trip. First, I got carsick in the airport limo. Then…

 Be sure to recycle this language.

Problems		**Responses**
The ___ was terrible.	Someone stole my ___ .	What was wrong with the ___ ?
The ___ were unfriendly.	The ___ drove me crazy.	I'm sorry to hear that.
They canceled my ___ .	The [flight] was bumpy / scary.	That's a shame / too bad.
The ___ didn't work.	The [drive] was long / boring.	
They lost my ___ .		

Review

A ◀») **Listening comprehension** It's 7:26 A.M. now. Listen as
you look at the departure board. Then listen again and use
reasoning to determine if each statement is true or false.
Circle T (true) or F (false).

T F **1** They could take the 8:31.

T F **2** They should take the 8:25.

T F **3** They're going to Boston.

T F **4** They're both going to take the train
to Washington.

T F **5** He usually takes the 7:25.

T F **6** They should hurry.

DEPARTURES		7:26 A.M.
TO	DEPARTS	TRACK
WASHINGTON	7:10	6
BOSTON	7:22	9
PHILADELPHIA	7:25	19
WASHINGTON	8:25	8
BOSTON	8:26	24
PHILADELPHIA	8:31	18

B Complete each statement with a correct word or phrase.

1 It's important to make a ....
early because it can be difficult to find a room
after you arrive.

2 When your whole family is going to the airport
together, you can reserve a ....
It's usually very comfortable and has space for all
of your luggage.

3 It can be convenient to use a .... if
you want to drive but can't bring your own car.

4 Do you think I should take the......................
train? I know it's much faster, but I'm not sure it
stops at my station on weekends.

5 My husband always gets ....
seat. He likes to get up and walk around on long
flights.

6 I hope it's a .... flight. I get really
scared every time the plane takes off or lands.

7 It's not a non-stop, but it's a......................
flight. You don't have to change planes, but the
plane stops twice.

8 Are you kidding? They .... it?
That was the last flight! Just ten minutes ago they
said it was here and ready to board!

9 The airline .... the flight, and
when I got to the gate, the agent said another
passenger had my seat. I had such bad luck!

5:18/5:19
Top Notch Pop
"Five Hundred Ways"
Lyrics p. 150

C Complete the conversation with <u>be going to</u> and the indicated verbs.

A: On Saturday, ... for Cancún.
                              1 we / leave

B: Really? .... a car there? There are some
                    2 you / rent
great places to explore.

A: No. I think .... on the beach and rest.
                          3 we / stay

By the way, where .... for your vacation?
                                    4 you and Margo / go

B: I'm not sure. But .... to Bangkok on
                          5 I / travel
business next month, and .... a few days
                                        6 I / take
off to go sightseeing. I hear it's great.

D **Writing** On a separate sheet of paper, write two paragraphs—one
about your most recent trip and one about your next trip. In the first
paragraph, describe the transportation you took and write about any
problems you had. In the second paragraph, write about the
transportation you plan to take. Use <u>be going to</u>.

WRITING BOOSTER ▸ p. 147

• *The paragraph*
• *Guidance for Exercise D*

Contest Form teams. Create questions about the trip to ask another team. (One point for each correct question and one point for each correct answer.)

Role play Choose one picture. Create a conversation for the people. Use <u>could</u> and <u>should</u>. For example:

Agent: You could go to Hawaii or ...

Group story Take turns telling the story in the pictures. Each student adds one sentence.

NOW I CAN...
- ☐ Discuss schedules and buy tickets.
- ☐ Book travel services.
- ☐ Understand airport announcements.
- ☐ Describe transportation problems.

Shopping Smart

GOALS After Unit 10, you will be able to

1 Ask for a recommendation.
2 Bargain for a lower price.
3 Discuss showing appreciation for service.
4 Describe where to get the best deals.

Exchange rate board (left column):

D	119 103
P	
AD	0.9978
NY	3.1
UR	0.6263
JPY	77
GD	13355
HKD	56
NZD	13247
MYR	37
THB	32.610
IDR	2.6

Get the Best Exchange Rate

Before you travel to another country, check the exchange rate of your currency against the currency of the foreign country you're visiting. During your trip, you'll get the best rate if you buy foreign currency with an ATM card or a credit card.

However, if you have to exchange cash, the best rates are usually at banks and post offices.

When possible, use a credit card for larger expenses such as hotel bills, tickets, and car rentals. But be careful—many credit card companies now add fees for these transactions. Use an ATM card for your daily cash needs. But check with your bank before you leave to make sure you can use your card in the country you are visiting. Also ask if they charge extra for using your card there.

VISTAcard

Monthly Statement

Date	Transaction	Debit
10/07	CAFÉ LUNA	200.00
10/06	*FOREIGN TRANSACTION FEE	4.68
10/06	HOTEL DE CALLAO	180.00

Source: independenttraveler.com

A 🔊 **Vocabulary** • *Financial terms*
Listen and repeat.

5:20

- an ATM
- cash
- foreign currency
- a currency exchange
- an exchange rate
- a fee

B **Pair work** Discuss your spending habits. Ask and answer the following questions.

1 Do you make purchases with a credit card? When?

2 What do you usually buy with cash?

3 Do you ever exchange money for foreign currency? When? How?

ENGLISH FOR TODAY'S WORLD
connecting people from different cultures
and language backgrounds

C 🔊 5:21 **Photo story** Read and listen to people shopping for souvenirs.

Jenn: Oh, no. I'm almost out of cash. And I want to get a gift for my mom. I sure hope these shops accept credit cards.

Pat: I'll bet they do. Let's go in here. They have some really nice stuff.

Jenn: Great!

Pat: Hey, what do you think of this?

Jenn: It's gorgeous. But it's a bit more than I want to spend.

Pat: Maybe you can get a better price. It can't hurt to ask.

Jenn: I don't know. I'm not very good at bargaining.

Clerk: Excuse me. Maybe I can help. Let me show you something more affordable.

Jenn: Oh, that one's nice, too. How much do you want for it?

Clerk: Well, the lowest I could go is forty euros.

Jenn: I'll take it. You do accept credit cards, don't you?

Clerk: Sorry, no. But there is an ATM right across the street.

Clerk: Italian speaker

D **Focus on language** Find an underlined statement in the Photo Story with the same meaning as each of the following:

1 I'd prefer something cheaper. ....

2 This shop sells good things. ....

3 I'll sell it to you for . . . .

4 I don't know how to ask for a lower price. ....

5 I don't have much money. ....

6 Don't be afraid to bargain. ....

7 Here's a cheaper one. ....

E **Discussion** Are you good at bargaining? How do you get a good price when you go shopping?

F **Pair work** Complete the chart with your own opinions of the advantages and disadvantages of credit cards and cash. Then discuss your ideas with a partner.

An advantage of credit cards:	
A disadvantage of credit cards:	
An advantage of cash:	
A disadvantage of cash:	

GOAL **Ask for a recommendation**

GRAMMAR *Superlative adjectives*

> **Irregular forms**
> good → better (than) → **the best**
> bad → worse (than) → **the worst**

Use superlative adjectives to compare more than two people, places, things, or ideas.

Which projector is **the cheapest** of these three?
Which brands are **the most popular** in your store?

adjective	comparative	superlative	adjective	comparative	superlative
cheap	cheaper (than)	**the cheapest**	comfortable	more comfortable (than)	**the most comfortable**
nice	nicer (than)	**the nicest**	portable	more portable (than)	**the most portable**
easy	easier (than)	**the easiest**	difficult	less difficult (than)	**the least difficult**
big	bigger (than)	**the biggest**	expensive	less expensive (than)	**the least expensive**

GRAMMAR BOOSTER ▸ p. 139

Comparatives and superlatives: usage and form

A Grammar practice Read the salesperson's recommendations. Complete each statement, using the superlative form of the adjective.

1 The Aptex is .... of our MP3 players.
   <small>new</small>

2 The Focus C20 is very inexpensive. It's .... digital camera we sell.
   <small>cheap</small>

3 Compared to our other camcorders, the Manko 210 is ....
   <small>easy to use</small>

4 The Focus C50 is .... digital camera we sell.
   <small>popular</small>

5 The Vista PX is .... camcorder you can buy.
   <small>light</small>

6 Our customers say the iSong is .... MP3 player available today.
   <small>practical</small>

7 You'll like the Manko 230 MP3 player. It's .... to use.
   <small>difficult</small>

8 If you don't want to spend a lot, the Raxx is .... camcorder you can buy.
   <small>expensive</small>

9 If you want the best but don't care about cost, the Vista LS is .... camcorder we have.
   <small>expensive</small>

B Complete the conversations. Use the superlative form of the adjectives.

1 A: All of these cameras are easy to use.
   B: But which is ....?
      <small>small</small>

2 A: All of our ski sweaters are pretty warm.
   B: But I want a really heavy one. Which brand makes .... ones?
      <small>heavy</small>

3 A: She wrote at least six books about Italy.
   B: I know. But which of her books is ....?
      <small>interesting</small>

4 A: Do you want to take a taxi, bus, or train to the airport?
   B: Which is ....?
      <small>convenient</small>

5 A: You can study English at any school you want.
   B: All three sound great. But which school is ....?
      <small>popular</small>

6 A: Here are three vacation packages you can choose from.
   B: That's nice. But just tell me which one is ....
      <small>affordable</small>

A 🔊 5:22 Read and listen to someone asking for a recommendation.

A: I'm looking for a digital camera. Which is the least expensive?

B: The B100. But it's not the best. How much can you spend?

A: No more than 250.

B: Well, we have some good ones in your price range.

A: Great! Can I have a look?

B 🔊 5:23 **Rhythm and intonation** Listen again and repeat. Then practice the Conversation Model with a partner.

NOW YOU CAN Ask for a recommendation

A Pair work Change the Conversation Model. Use the ads, or other real ads, to ask for a recommendation. Use superlative adjectives. Then change roles.

A: I'm looking for .... Which is the ....?

B: The .... But it's not the .... How much can you spend?

A: No more than ....

B: Well, ...

A: ....

Ideas
• nice
• popular
• light
• practical
• easy to use

> **Don't stop! Continue the conversation.**
> I'm also looking for [an MP3 player].
> Tell me about [the Prego 5].
> Do you accept credit cards?
> Is there an ATM nearby?
> I think I'll take the [X23].
> Could you gift wrap it for me?

B Change partners Ask about other electronic products.

C Extension Bring in newspaper ads for electronic and other products. Use both comparative and superlative adjectives to discuss them.

MP3 Players

Rico SL-S225 **$129**
Practical

Pusan X23
$109
Easy to Use

Power X
Music Master
NEW **$199**

Camcorders

Vision 720 **$949**
Very Light

Pusan 5X
$829
Easy to Use

Diego P500
$299
Popular

Digital Cameras

Honshu X24
$209
Very Popular

Honshu B100
$149

Prego 5
$299
NEW

GOAL Bargain for a lower price

CONVERSATION MODEL

A 🔊 5:24 Read and listen to someone bargaining for a lower price.

A: How much do you want for that rug?

B: This one?

A: No. That one's not big enough. The other one.

B: 300.

A: That's a lot more than I want to spend. I can give you 200.

B: How about 225?

A: OK. That sounds fair.

B 🔊 5:25 **Rhythm and intonation** Listen again and repeat. Then practice the Conversation Model with a partner.

GRAMMAR   *Too* and *enough*

When something is not satisfactory:

Those rugs are **too small**.   OR   Those rugs aren**'t big enough**.
That camera is **too heavy**.   OR   That camera isn**'t light enough**.

When something is satisfactory:

This MP3 player is **small enough**. I'll take it.

Be careful!

Don't say: This MP3 player is ~~enough small~~.

> **GRAMMAR BOOSTER** ▸ p. 140
> • Usage: *too*, *really*, and *very*

Grammar practice Read the conversations between customers and salespeople. Then complete each conversation. Use *too* or *enough* and an adjective from the list.

1 A: Are you sure this microwave is ....? I'm a pretty busy guy.
B: Absolutely. The X11 is our fastest model.

2 A: These shoes aren't .... They're very uncomfortable.
B: I'm so sorry. Let me get you a bigger size.

3 A: My photocopier is .... It's driving me crazy!
B: Then let me show you a model that's quieter.

4 A: I bought these portable speakers last week, but they really aren't
.... for travel.
B: Don't worry. You can exchange them for another pair that's not so heavy.

5 A: How about this MP3 player? It's pretty small.
B: That's definitely .... I'll take it.

6 A: This jacket is a real bargain, sir. It's only $692.
B: $692? That's .... I don't want to spend that much.

Adjectives
slow
fast
cheap
expensive
quiet
noisy
small
big
light
heavy

Rising intonation for clarification

A 🔊 5:26 Listen to how rising intonation is used to ask for clarification. Then listen again and repeat.

1 A: Could I have a look at those bowls?

B: These small ones?

A: No, the big ones.

2 A: How much is that vase?

B: This green one?

A: That's right.

B **Pair work** Place some objects on your desk. Ask to have a look, and practice using rising intonation to ask for clarification.

66 Could I have a look at those sunglasses? 99

66 These brown ones? 99

How to bargain

A 🔊 5:27 Read and listen. Then listen again and repeat.

Buyer's language
• **How much do you want for that** [shawl]?
• **That's more than I want to spend.**
• **I can give you** [twenty] **for it.**
• **Would you take** [thirty]?
• **All I have is** [forty].
• **It's a deal.**

Seller's language
• **How much do you want to spend?**
• **I could go as low as** [seventy].
• **I can't go lower than** [sixty].
• **You can have it for** [fifty].
• **How about** [forty-five]?
• **It's a deal.**

B 🔊 5:28 **Listening comprehension** Listen to people bargaining. Complete each statement with the amount they agreed on and the item bought.

1 The buyer pays …….. for the …………… .

2 The buyer pays …….. for the …………… .

3 The buyer pays …….. for the …………… .

4 The buyer pays …….. for the …………… .

NOW YOU CAN **Bargain for a lower price**

A **Role play** Imagine that you are in a place where bargaining is common. One of you is the buyer, and the other is the seller. Use the Vocabulary and the photos, or your own ideas. Then change roles. Start like this:

A: How much do you want for …….. ?

Don't stop!
• Ask about size, color, etc.
• Use <u>too</u> and <u>enough</u>.
• Use superlatives.

B **Change partners** Bargain for one of the other items.

GOAL Discuss showing appreciation for service

Warm-up In your opinion, why is it important to understand the customs of other countries?

When Should I Tip?
It's the question every traveler asks.

In some countries around the world, tipping isn't customary. But there are at least 180 countries where travelers need to know the rules. In some places, like China, where tipping was not the custom in the past, that's changing. In most other countries, tipping is customary—but the rules can be quite complicated.

Restaurants

In the U.S., restaurant servers expect a tip of 15 to 20% of the check—depending on how satisfied you are with the service. In most other countries, however, it's about 10%. In the U.S., you leave your tip on the table. But in Austria and Germany, it's considered rude if you don't hand the tip directly to the server.

In Europe, restaurants almost always add a service charge to the check, so you don't need to leave a separate tip. But in the U.S., a service charge is only added for groups of six or more people. So it's a good idea to look carefully at your check!

And if that's not complicated enough, think about this: In some countries, like Italy and Venezuela, restaurants add a service charge to the bill, but an additional 5 to 10% tip is still expected!

Taxis

In the U.S. and Canada, you always tip taxi drivers 15% of the taxi fare. However, in South America and many European countries, you don't usually tip them. Instead, you can round off the fare and say, "Keep the change."

Hotels

What about the porter who carries your luggage? In Australia, you tip about AUS $3 (US $2) per bag. But in most countries, a tip of about US $1 will be fine. You can also leave about US $1 to $2 a day for the maid who cleans your hotel room.

So what should travelers do? Check the Internet for information on tipping customs before you leave. As the famous saying goes, "When in Rome, do as the Romans do." But remember: You never have to tip if the service is terrible.

FOR YOUR INFORMATION

Never tip in these countries:

Japan	Singapore
Korea	Thailand
Malaysia	United Arab Emirates
New Zealand	Vietnam

Information source: cnn.com

A **Draw conclusions** Read each person's question. Give advice, according to the Reading. Then find the place in the Reading where the information comes from.

> 66 I'm going to Warsaw, Poland. I'm staying in a nice hotel for about six days. How much should I tip the maid? 99

> 66 I'm going to Chicago, in the U.S., on business. Let's say I take ten clients out for lunch and the bill is US $400. How much more should I leave for the tip? 99

> 66 I'm flying to Melbourne, Australia, next week. I have three large bags. If a porter helps me, how much should I tip? 99

> 66 I'm going to be in Toronto, Canada, this weekend. Someone told me the fare from the airport is CAN $43. How much should I tip the driver? 99

B **Apply information** Imagine that you are visiting one of the countries in the Reading. Describe a situation in a restaurant, a hotel, or a taxi. Your classmates decide how much to tip.

> On your *ActiveBook* Self-Study Disc:
> **Extra Reading Comprehension Questions**

NOW YOU CAN   Discuss showing appreciation for service

A **Frame your ideas** Check the ways you have shown appreciation to someone for good service. Then tell a partner about some of them.

- ☐ I left a tip.
- ☐ I gave a gift.
- ☐ I said "Thank you."
- ☐ I wrote a "thank-you" note.
- ☐ I wrote a letter to the manager.
- ☐ Other: _____

> 66 Last year, I went to a restaurant where the waiter was really nice. At the end of the meal, I spoke to the manager about his great service. 99

B **Notepadding** With a partner, write suggestions to a visitor to your country for how to show appreciation for good service. If tipping is customary, explain how much to tip.

Restaurant servers:	
Taxi drivers:	
Hotel maids:	
Baggage porters:	
Hairdressers:	
Office assistants:	
Other:	

C **Discussion** Now discuss how to show appreciation for good service in your country. What are the customs? Does everyone agree?

> **Text-mining** (optional)
> Underline language in the Reading on page 116 to use in the Discussion. For example:
> "[Restaurant servers] expect a tip of …"

GOAL | **Describe where to get the best deals**

BEFORE YOU LISTEN

A 🔊 5:30 **Vocabulary** • *How to describe good and bad deals* Read and listen. Then listen again and repeat.

Good deals

She **got a great deal**.
She **saved a lot of money**.
It **was a real bargain**.

Bad deals

He **got a bad deal**.
He **paid too much money**.
It **was a total rip-off**.

B Discussion Read about two shopping experiences. Do you think either of the people got a good deal? Use the Vocabulary.

I was in Saudi Arabia on business, and I wanted to buy a rug. I found a beautiful one, but the asking price was too high: US $900. I said I could go as high as $350. We bargained for a long time, but the merchant wouldn't come down in price. Finally, we shook hands. When I turned to leave the store, he was very surprised. I thought the handshake meant "Sorry. That's too low." But it really meant "It's a deal." So I went back in and bought it.

When I was in Shanghai, I decided to look for some antique pottery. I found a beautiful blue and white vase from the sixteenth-century Ming Dynasty. We bargained about the price, and the salesperson came way down for me. So of course I bought it. It was more than I wanted to spend, but I really liked it. Later, a friend told me that the "antiques" in these shops aren't really antiques—they're actually new!

LISTENING COMPREHENSION

A 🔊 5:31 **Listen for main ideas** Listen to the conversations about shopping. Then listen again and complete the chart.

	What did the shopper buy?	Did the shopper get a good price?	
1		☐ yes	☐ no
2		☐ yes	☐ no
3		☐ yes	☐ no
4		☐ yes	☐ no

B 🔊 **Listen for details** Listen again. Write the price each person paid.

1 .... euros   2 .... pounds   3 .... dollars   4 .... pesos

NOW YOU CAN   Describe where to get the best deals

A Notepadding Write notes about a good or bad shopping experience you have had.

What did you buy?	
Where did you buy it?	
Did you bargain?	
How much did you pay?	

B Group work Now describe your shopping experience to your classmates. Use your notepad.

Text-mining (optional)
Underline language in the stories in Exercise B on page 118 to use in the Group Work. For example:

"We bargained for a long time ..."

C Frame your ideas Complete the chart with places in your city or town.

What are . . .	Where can you buy . . .
the best restaurants?	the least expensive fruits and vegetables?
the nicest hotels?	the most beautiful flowers?
the most expensive department stores?	the best electronic products?
the most unusual markets?	the most unusual souvenirs?
the most interesting museums?	the wildest clothes?

D Discussion Where should people go in your city or town for the best deals?

❝ The fruits and vegetables at the North Market are the freshest in town. ❞

Review

A 🔊 **Listening comprehension** Listen to each conversation. Write the item that the people are talking about. Indicate whether the item is satisfactory (✓) or unsatisfactory (✗) to the customer. Then listen again and circle the adjectives that the salesperson uses to describe the product.

	They're talking about . . .	Satisfactory?	Adjectives
1		☐	light / fast / cheap
2		☐	light / warm / beautiful
3		☐	tall / beautiful / affordable
4		☐	light / easy to use / affordable

B Complete the sentences.

1 If you're out of cash and the bank is closed, you can get money from ....

2 If there's a service charge on the bill, you probably don't need to leave ....

3 In some places, you can .... for a lower price.

4 Before you go overseas, you should check the .... of your currency and the currency of the place you're traveling.

5 It was a real .... I saved a lot of money.

6 It was a total .... I paid too much money.

C On a separate sheet of paper, rewrite each sentence, using <u>too</u> or <u>enough</u>. For example:

That vase is too heavy.

> *That vase isn't light enough.*

1 Those cameras aren't cheap enough.

2 This printer is too slow.

3 The inside of the fridge isn't cool enough.

4 That restaurant is too noisy.

5 My flat screen TV isn't big enough.

6 Those pants aren't long enough.

D Write two sentences about shopping in your city. Use the superlative.

> *The stores in Old Town have the most interesting gifts.*

1 _____

2 _____

5:34/5:35

Top Notch Pop
"Shopping for Souvenirs"
Lyrics p. 150

E **Writing** On a separate sheet of paper, write a guide to the best places for a visitor to your city or town to stay in, visit, and shop.

Ideas

hotels	theaters
stores	neighborhoods
museums	stadiums

WRITING BOOSTER ▶ p. 148

• *Connecting contradictory ideas*
• *Guidance for Exercise E*

Al's Electronics

SALE!

CoolRay 6
Super thin
US $350

Now US $220
Easy to use
Only 3 oz / .085 kg

Basik XT
So Fast!
US $980

Now US $950
Very Professional
Only 24 oz / .68 kg

EasyPix 500
Very Popular
US $220
Now US $180
Only 4.1 oz / .12 kg

SALE!

Dazio 420
Brightness: 2000 lumens
Very portable
US $1,199

Now US $999
Only 2.8 lb / 1.27 kg

Clearview 3Z
Brightness: 2000 lumens
Really affordable
US $899

Now US $849
Only 4 lb / 1.81 kg

Manna T-20
Brightness: 4000 lumens
So powerful!
US $3,999

Now US $3,899
Only 3.5 lb / 1.59 kg

SALE!

Cloud 9
50"/ 127 cm
Like it loud? This is the one!
US $1,399

Now US $1,149

Runex
19"/ 48 cm
Very portable
US $399

Now US $229

Washburn
32"/ 81 cm
Brand new!
US $699

Now US $599

ORAL REVIEW

Contest Form teams. Create false statements about the products. Another team corrects the statements. (Teams get one point for each statement they correct.) For example:

There's a sale on camcorders today.

Role play Create conversations for the people.
- Ask for a recommendation. Start like this:
  I'm looking for ___. Which is the . . . ?
- Bargain for the best price. Start like this:
  How much do you want for that . . . ?

GIFTS 'N THINGS

NOW I CAN...
- [ ] Ask for a recommendation.
- [ ] Bargain for a lower price.
- [ ] Discuss showing appreciation for service.
- [ ] Describe where to get the best deals.

121

Reference Charts

Countries and nationalities

Argentina	Argentinean / Argentine	Guatemala	Guatemalan	Peru	Peruvian
Australia	Australian	Holland	Dutch	Poland	Polish
Belgium	Belgian	Honduras	Honduran	Portugal	Portuguese
Bolivia	Bolivian	Hungary	Hungarian	Russia	Russian
Brazil	Brazilian	India	Indian	Saudi Arabia	Saudi / Saudi Arabian
Canada	Canadian	Indonesia	Indonesian	Spain	Spanish
Chile	Chilean	Ireland	Irish	Sweden	Swedish
China	Chinese	Italy	Italian	Switzerland	Swiss
Colombia	Colombian	Japan	Japanese	Taiwan	Chinese
Costa Rica	Costa Rican	Korea	Korean	Thailand	Thai
Ecuador	Ecuadorian	Lebanon	Lebanese	Turkey	Turkish
Egypt	Egyptian	Malaysia	Malaysian	the United Kingdom	British
El Salvador	Salvadorean	Mexico	Mexican	the United States	American
France	French	Nicaragua	Nicaraguan	Uruguay	Uruguayan
Germany	German	Panama	Panamanian	Venezuela	Venezuelan
Greece	Greek	Paraguay	Paraguayan	Vietnam	Vietnamese

Non-count nouns

This list is an at-a-glance reference to the non-count nouns used in *Top Notch 1*.

aerobics	cheese	entertainment	ice	oil	service	traffic
air-conditioning	chicken	fish	ice cream	outerwear	shopping	transportation
basketball	clothing	food	juice	pasta	shrimp	TV
beef	coffee	fruit	junk food	pepper	sightseeing	walking
bike riding	crab	garlic	lamb	pie	skydiving	water
bread	culture	golf	lettuce	rice	sleepwear	weather
broccoli	dancing	health	lingerie	running	soccer	wildlife
butter	dessert	history	meat	salad	soup	yogurt
cake	dinner	hosiery	milk	salt	squid	
candy	electronics	hot sauce	music	sausage	swimming	
cash	English	housework	nature	seafood	tennis	

Irregular verbs

base form	simple past	past participle	base form	simple past	past participle	base form	simple past	past participle
be	was / were	been	give	gave	given	sell	sold	sold
begin	began	begun	go	went	gone	send	sent	sent
break	broke	broken	grow	grew	grown	shake	shook	shaken
bring	brought	brought	have	had	had	sing	sang	sung
build	built	built	hear	heard	heard	sit	sat	sat
buy	bought	bought	hit	hit	hit	sleep	slept	slept
catch	caught	caught	hurt	hurt	hurt	speak	spoke	spoken
choose	chose	chosen	keep	kept	kept	spend	spent	spent
come	came	come	know	knew	known	stand	stood	stood
cost	cost	cost	leave	left	left	steal	stole	stolen
cut	cut	cut	lose	lost	lost	swim	swam	swum
do	did	done	make	made	made	take	took	taken
drink	drank	drunk	mean	meant	meant	teach	taught	taught
drive	drove	driven	meet	met	met	tell	told	told
eat	ate	eaten	pay	paid	paid	think	thought	thought
fall	fell	fallen	put	put	put	throw	threw	thrown
feel	felt	felt	quit	quit	quit	understand	understood	understood
find	found	found	read	read	read	wake up	woke up	woken up
fit	fit	fit	ride	rode	ridden	wear	wore	worn
fly	flew	flown	run	ran	run	win	won	won
forget	forgot	forgotten	say	said	said	write	wrote	written
get	got	gotten	see	saw	seen			

Grammar Booster

The Grammar Booster is optional. It is not required for the achievement tests in the *Top Notch Complete Assessment Package*. If you use the Grammar Booster, there are extra exercises in the Workbook in a separate labeled Grammar Booster section.

UNIT 1 Lesson 1

Information questions with be: usage and form

Use <u>Who</u> to ask about people, <u>What</u> to ask about things, <u>Where</u> to ask about places, and <u>How old</u> to ask about age.

singular nouns	plural nouns
Who's your teacher?	Who **are** the new students?
What's your name?	What **are** their names?
Where's your father from?	Where **are** your classmates from?
How old **is** your sister?	How old **are** your children?

A Choose an answer for each question.

___ 1 What's your name?

___ 2 Where is she from?

___ 3 Where's her father from?

___ 4 Who is Bernard Udall?

___ 5 How old are your cousins?

a Scotland, actually. She's British.

b He's the CEO of BRC Incorporated.

c Kim's father? Seoul, I think.

d Eighteen and ten.

e Ivan. But everyone calls me Vanya.

Possessive nouns and adjectives

Possessive nouns

Add <u>'s</u> to a name or a noun.
Where is **Peter's** father from? What's the **teacher's** name?

Add an apostrophe (') to plural nouns that end in -s.
What are the **students'** names?

Add <u>'s</u> to the name or noun that comes last in a list of two or more.
When is **Sally and Hannah's** class?

Possessive adjectives
Where's Chad's father from? → Where's **his** father from?
What's Sheila's last name? → What's **her** last name?
What's Lee and Ping's address? → What's **their** address?

I → **my**
you → **your**
he → **his**
she → **her**
it → **its**
we → **our**
they → **their**

B Complete each sentence with a possessive form of the noun.

1 _____ (Dean) father is an engineer.

2 What is _____ (Janec) e-mail address?

3 The book is _____ (Kayla).

4 _____ (Nicole and Sean) class is at eight.

5 What are your _____ (brothers) occupations?

C On a separate sheet of paper, write a question for each answer, using <u>What</u> and a possessive adjective. Follow the example.

My occupation? I'm a student. *What's your occupation?*

1 Lin and Ben's? It's 2 Bay Street.

2 His phone number? It's 21-66-55.

3 Dave's last name? It's Bourne.

4 Sandra's nickname? It's Sandy.

5 My e-mail address? It's acme4@ymail.com.

6 Ray's? His address is 456 Rue Noire.

D Complete each sentence with a possessive adjective.

1 This is my sister. _____ husband is from Ecuador.

2 Robert is a new student here. _____ nickname is Bobby.

3 My friends live in London, but _____ hometown is in Scotland.

4 My husband and I live in Chicago, but _____ children don't.

5 I'd like you to meet _____ colleague Sam. He works with me at the bank.

6 I like that picture. _____ colors are very nice.

UNIT 1   Lesson 2

Verb be: usage and form

The verb <u>be</u> gives information about the subject of a sentence. The subject of a sentence can be a noun or a pronoun.

noun subject
Our teacher is from the United States.
That school is new.

pronoun subject
She is from the United States.
It is new.

Affirmative statements
There are three forms of the verb <u>be</u> in the present tense: <u>am</u>, <u>is</u>, and <u>are</u>.

I **am** a student.

He
She ⎦ **is** late.
It

You
We ⎦ **are** married.
They

Contracted forms
Contract <u>be</u> with subject nouns and pronouns. Use contractions in speaking and informal writing.

Robin is an artist. = **Robin's** an artist.
He is single. = **He's** single.

I am a student. = **I'm** a student.
You are on time. = **You're** on time.

Negative contractions
There are two ways to form negative contractions.

He's **not** Brazilian. = He **isn't** Brazilian.
They're **not** teachers. = They **aren't** teachers.

Note: There is only one way to contract <u>I am not</u> → I'm not.

Short answers with be: common errors

Don't use contractions with affirmative short answers to <u>yes</u> / <u>no</u> questions.

Are you a salesperson?   Yes, I am. NOT ~~Yes, I'm.~~
Is he American?   Yes, he is. NOT ~~Yes, he's.~~
Are they designers?   Yes, they are. NOT ~~Yes, they're.~~

Note: It is also common to answer just with <u>Yes</u> or <u>No</u>.
Are you a salesperson?   Yes.

A On a separate sheet of paper, write these sentences, using contractions. Then practice saying each sentence aloud.

1 She is an opera singer.
2 They are managers.
3 I am a student.
4 Bart is from Australia.
5 My mother is late.
6 Your father is nice.

B On a separate sheet of paper, write a short answer for each question.

1 Is New York in Russia?
2 Are you a scientist?
3 Are Korea and Japan in Asia?
4 Is Italy a city?
5 Is it 3:00 right now?
6 Are you a student?
7 Are you Canadian?
8 Is your father a manager?
9 Is English difficult?

Prepositions of time and place: usage rules

Time

Use <u>on</u> with the names of days or dates.

on Thursday	on Monday morning	on New Year's Day
on the weekend	on Sundays	on a weekday

Use <u>in</u> with periods of time (but not with names of days).

in 2008	in July	in [the] spring	in an hour
in the morning	in the 20th century	in the 1950s	in two weeks

Use <u>at</u> with specific moments in time.

at 9:00	at dawn	at noon
at sunrise	at dusk	at midnight

Place

Use <u>on</u> with the names of streets and specific physical locations.

on Main Street	on Smith Avenue	on the corner
on the street	on the right	on the left

Use <u>in</u> with the names of cities, countries, continents, and other large locations.

in the neighborhood	in the center of town	in Lima
in Korea	in Africa	in the ocean

Use <u>at</u> for buildings and addresses.

at the theater	at the supermarket	at the bank
at the train station	at 10 Main Street	

A Complete the following sentences with <u>on</u>, <u>in</u>, or <u>at</u>.

1 When's the movie? The movie is _____ Friday _____ 8:30.

2 _____ the weekend, I'm going to the concert _____ the public library.

3 Where is he? He's not here right now. He's _____ work.

4 Where's his office? It's _____ the center of town.

5 When was her mother born? She was born _____ January 1.

6 When does the movie take place? It takes place _____ the 19th century _____ Africa.

7 The park opens _____ 6:00 _____ the morning and closes _____ dusk.

8 Is the concert hall _____ Grove Street?

9 I think the theater is _____ the right side of the street.

10 Let's go to the evening show. The concert is outside, and the weather is really hot _____ the afternoon.

11 This concert occurs every second year _____ November.

12 I'll see you _____ Thursday morning in front of the theater, OK?

B Look at the tickets. On a separate sheet of paper, write questions with <u>When</u> or <u>What time</u>. Write a question with <u>Where</u>.

The simple present tense: usage and form

Usage

Use the simple present tense to talk about facts and habitual actions in the present.

facts	habitual actions
Josh **speaks** Spanish very well.	Josh **speaks** Spanish every day.
They **work** at Coffee Central.	They **work** late on Fridays.

Form

Add **-s** to the base form of the verb for third-person singular (**he**, **she**, or **it**).

I **like** Thai food.	He **likes** Peruvian food.
You **study** English.	She **studies** French.
They **open** at 6:00.	The store **opens** at 8:00.
We **work** at a café.	Marlene **works** at a school.

Negative forms

Use **don't** (**do not**) and **doesn't** (**does not**) + the base form of a verb to make negative statements.

I **don't like** American food.	He **doesn't like** Greek food.

Yes / no questions

Use **do** or **does** + the base form of a verb to form **yes / no** questions.

Do you **speak** Portuguese?	**Does** she **speak** French? NOT Does she ~~speaks~~ French?

A **Write negative statements. Follow the example.**

Gwen likes classical music. (Her sister) _Her sister doesn't like classical music._

1 The café closes at 6:00. (The bookstore) _____

2 Neal lives in Quito. (His sister) _____

3 Miles works in an office. (His brother) _____

4 I have a big family. (My husband) _____

5 My younger brother speaks Chinese. (I) _____

6 Kiko's nephew likes hip-hop. (Her niece) _____

B **Write yes / no questions. Follow the example.**

A: _Does your sister live_ near you? B: No, she doesn't. She lives in another city.

1 A: _____ drink coffee?
   B: No, he doesn't. My brother drinks tea.

2 A: _____ children?
   B: No, we don't have any yet.

3 A: _____ in Mexico?
   B: No, my in-laws live in Chile.

4 A: _____ English?
   B: Yes, she does. My niece speaks it well.

5 A: _____ work here?
   B: Yes, they do. My cousins work downstairs.

6 A: _____ early?
   B: No. The bookstore opens late.

Information questions in the simple present tense: form and common errors

Do and does
Use do or does + the base form of a verb to ask information questions.

Where **do** your in-laws **live**?   Where **does** your sister **live**?
When **do** you **visit** your parents?   When **does** she **visit** her parents?
How often **do** they **go** to class?   How often **does** he **go** to class?

Questions with who
Compare these questions with who.

                                                                      subject
Who visits your cousin in Chicago?   **My mother** does.

                                                                      object
Who does your mother visit in Chicago?   My mother visits **my cousin**.

Be careful! Don't use do or does with Who if the question is about the subject. Always use the third-person singular form to ask questions with Who about the subject.

Who **lives** here? NOT Who ~~does live~~ here? NOT Who ~~live~~ here?

How many
Be careful! Always use How many with plural nouns.

How many cousins do you have? NOT How many ~~cousin~~ do you have?

Complete the information questions.

1 _____ your father _____? He's a doctor.
2 _____ your in-laws _____? They live in Seoul.
3 _____ cousins _____? I have ten of them.
4 _____ your parents? I visit them every weekend.
5 _____ your sister _____? She lives across the street.
6 _____ speaks Russian? My brother-in-law does.
7 _____ your aunt _____ with? She lives with my cousin.
8 _____ you _____? I study late at night.
9 _____ has three kids? My sister does.
10 _____ your older brother _____? He studies in London.

Non-count nouns: categories and verb agreement

Non-count nouns are common in the following categories:
  abstract ideas: health, advice, help, luck, fun
  sports and activities: tennis, swimming, golf, basketball
  illnesses: cancer, AIDS, diabetes, dengue
  academic subjects: English, chemistry, art, mathematics
  foods: rice, milk, sugar, coffee, fat

All non-count nouns require a singular verb.
  Fat **isn't** good for you.
  Mathematics **is** my favorite subject.

A Complete each sentence with the correct form of the verb.

1 Coffee _____ (be) my favorite beverage.

2 Rice _____ (be) very good for you, even when you are sick.

3 Mathematics _____ (create) problems for many students, but not for me!

4 Influenza _____ (cause) pain and fever.

5 Darkness _____ (frighten) some people, but I don't know why.

6 Medical advice _____ (help) people decide what to do about their health.

B Complete the following sentences with _a_ or _an_. If the noun is a non-count noun, write an X.

1 He has _____ diabetes.

2 She would like to eat _____ banana.

3 "_____ apple a day keeps the doctor away."

4 Would you like _____ appetizer?

5 There's _____ egg on the shelf.

6 Does the restaurant serve _____ rice with the chicken?

7 He always gives _____ good advice.

8 My family loves _____ music.

Non-count nouns: expressing quantities

We can make many non-count nouns countable:
a slice of bread, a loaf of bread, three pieces of bread, two kinds of bread

The following phrases are used with non-count nouns in order to make them countable:
liquids: a glass of, two cups of, a liter of, six gallons of, a bottle of, a can of
solids: a cup of, a piece of, three slices of, a kilo of, a spoonful of

---

C On a separate sheet of paper, complete each statement with a countable quantity. (Note: More than one phrase of quantity may be possible.)

liquids

1 This soup is so creamy. It has two ___ milk in it.

2 She must be very thirsty. This is her third ___ water.

3 My car has a big gas tank. It holds ___ gas.

solids

4 I ate ___ cheese and now I feel sick.

5 A club sandwich doesn't have two ___ bread. It has three ___ bread.

6 I like my tea sweet. Please put in ___ sugar.

Questions with _How much_ and _How many_

Ask questions with _How much_ for non-count nouns. Ask questions with _How many_ for count nouns.

How much rice is in the soup?   Not much. Two cups.
How many eggs are in the fridge?   Not many. Three.

D Complete each question with _How much_ or _How many_.

1 _____ bread do we need?

2 _____ salt did you put in the beef stew?

3 _____ hot pepper do you like?

4 _____ spoonfuls of sugar do you want in your tea?

5 _____ oil should I put in this salad?

6 _____ cheese is there in the fridge?

7 _____ slices of bread do you want?

8 _____ cups of coffee did you drink?

Words that can be count nouns or non-count nouns

Some nouns can be used as count or non-count nouns. The word is the same, but the meaning is different.

non-count use	count use
Chicken is delicious.	I bought two chickens.
Let's watch TV.	We have three TVs in our house.
The sun provides light.	It's too bright in here. Turn off one of the lights.

Some words can have a count sense or a non-count sense without any real difference in meaning.
I'm in the mood for salad. OR I'm in the mood for a salad.
I'd like steak for dinner. OR I'd like a steak for dinner.

Plural count nouns: spelling rules

Add -s to most nouns.

cup **cups**   appetizer **appetizers**   apple **apples**

If a noun ends in a consonant and -y, change the y to i and add -es.

cherry **cherries**   berry **berries**

BUT: Do not change the y when the letter before the y is a vowel.

boy **boys**

Add -es to nouns that end in -ch, -o, -s, -sh, -x, or -z.

lunch **lunches**   radish **radishes**   tomato **tomatoes**
box **boxes**   glass **glasses**

E Write the plural form of the following count nouns.

1 clam _____   4 olive _____   7 french fry _____

2 snack _____   5 spoonful _____   8 sandwich _____

3 cup _____   6 pear _____   9 vegetable _____

                                                   10 potato _____

UNIT 4   Lesson 2

Some and any

Use some and any to describe an indefinite number or amount.

There are **some** apples in the fridge. (Indefinite number: we don't know how many.)
Are there **any** oranges? (Indefinite number: no specific number being asked about.)
They are bringing us **some** coffee. (Indefinite amount: we don't know how much.)

Use some with non-count nouns and with plural count nouns in affirmative statements.

     non-count noun   plural count noun
We need **some** milk and **some** bananas.

Use any with non-count nouns and plural count nouns in negative statements.

     non-count noun   plural count noun
We don't want **any** cheese, and we don't need **any** apples.

Use any or some in questions with count and non-count nouns. There is no difference in meaning.

Do you need **any** cookies or butter?   Do you need **some** cookies or butter?

A Change the following sentences from affirmative to negative. Follow the example.

There is some coffee in the kitchen. _There isn't any coffee in the kitchen._

1 There are some onions on the table. _____

2 We have some cookies. _____

3 They need some onions for the soup. _____

4 She's buying some fruit at the market. _____

5 The Reeds want some eggs for breakfast. _____

6 I want some butter on my sandwich. _____

7 There is some chicken in the fridge. _____

8 They need some cheese for the pasta. _____

B Complete each sentence with some or any.

1 I don't want _____ more coffee, thank you.

2 There isn't _____ salt in this soup.

3 We don't see _____ sandwiches on the menu.

4 They need _____ sugar for their tea.

5 The restaurant is making _____ pies for the party.

6 It's too bad that there isn't _____ soup.

7 I don't see _____ menus on those tables.

8 There are _____ eggs for the omelette.

The present continuous: spelling rules for the present participle

The present continuous consists of two parts: a form of <u>be</u> and a present participle of a verb.
To form a present participle, add <u>-ing</u> to the base form of a verb.

base form	present participle
talk	→ talk**ing**

If the base form ends in a silent (unvoiced) <u>-e</u>, drop the <u>-e</u> and add <u>-ing</u>.

leave   →   leav**ing**

In verbs of one syllable, if the last three letters are a consonant-vowel-consonant* sequence, double the last consonant and then add <u>-ing</u> to the base form.

C V C
s i t   →   sit**ting**

BUT: If the base form of the verb ends in <u>-w</u>, <u>-x</u>, or <u>-y</u>, don't double the final consonant.

blow   →   **blowing**
fix   →   **fixing**
say   →   **saying**

* **Vowels** = a, e, i, o, u
* **Consonants** = b, c, d, f, g, h, j, k, l, m, n, p, q, r, s, t, v, w, x, y, z

If a base form has more than one syllable and ends in a consonant-vowel-consonant sequence, double the last consonant only if the spoken stress is on the last syllable.

per - mit   →   permit**ting**   BUT or - der →   ordering

A Write the present participle for each of the following base forms. Follow the rules.

1 turn _____	**7** stop _____	**13** sew _____	**19** change _____
2 rain _____	**8** exit _____	**14** listen _____	**20** be _____
3 run _____	**9** sit _____	**15** do _____	**21** have _____
4 help _____	**10** eat _____	**16** write _____	**22** put _____
5 open _____	**11** buy _____	**17** begin _____	**23** go _____
6 close _____	**12** mix _____	**18** use _____	**24** pay _____

The present continuous: rules for forming statements

Remember to form the present continuous with <u>be</u> and a present participle of a verb.

affirmative statements	negative statements
I'm **studying** English.	I'm not **studying** French.
You're **studying** French.	You're not **studying** English.
He's **reading** a book.	He's not **reading** a newspaper.
She's **reading** a newspaper.	She's not **reading** a book.
We're **watching** TV.	We're not **watching** a DVD.
They're **watching** a video.	They're not **watching** TV.

B On a separate sheet of paper, change each affirmative statement to a negative statement. Use contractions.

1 She's going to the supermarket.

2 He's calling his wife this afternoon.

3 I'm cooking dinner tonight.

4 The Roberts are feeding their kids early.

5 Joel's taking the bus to the movies.

6 We're getting a new printer.

C Write answers to the following questions in complete affirmative or negative statements. Use the present continuous and contractions.

1 Are you studying English this weekend? _____

2 When are you taking a vacation? _____

3 Is it raining now? _____

4 Where are you eating dinner tonight? _____

5 Are you listening to music now? _____

6 Who's making breakfast tomorrow? _____

The present continuous: rules for forming questions

Yes / no questions: Place a form of be before the subject of the sentence. (Invert the subject and verb be.)

Is she watching TV?   **Are we** meeting this afternoon?
Are you driving there?   **Are they** talking on the phone?
Is Stu shopping?   **Are Nan and Bert** studying?

Information questions: Use question words to ask information questions. (Invert the subject and verb be.)

When are you going?   **How much** are you paying for that computer?
What are you doing right now?   **Why** are you buying that laptop?
Who is he watching on TV?

Be careful with Who when asking a question about the subject:

Who's talking on the phone? (John is.)

D Write a question in the present continuous to complete each conversation.

1. A: _____?
   B: No. Luke's not watching TV right now.

2 A: _____?
   B: Yes, She's working this morning.

3 A: _____?
   B: I'm calling Janet Hammond.

4 A: _____?
   B: She's coming home later tonight.

UNIT 6   *Lesson 1*

Can and have to: form and common errors

Be careful! Use can with the base form of a verb.

She **can play** golf very well.   **Can** he **play** tennis?
NOT ~~She cans play.~~   NOT ~~Cans he play?~~
NOT ~~She can plays.~~   NOT ~~Can he plays?~~
NOT ~~She can to play.~~   NOT ~~Can he to play?~~

There are three negative forms of can.

He **can't** swim. = He **cannot** swim. = He **can not** swim.

Use have to or has to with the base form of a verb.

I
You   } **have to go** to class at 9:00.   She } **has to go** to class at 8:00.
They   He
We

Be careful!

It **has to close** at 4:00.   **Does** he **have to go**?
NOT ~~It has to closes.~~   NOT ~~Does he have to goes?~~
NOT ~~It has to closing.~~   NOT ~~Does he has to go?~~

A Correct the following sentences.

1 Can they ~~coming~~ come to the movie next week?

2 My mother-in-law have to go shopping this afternoon.

3 My cousin can't plays soccer tomorrow.

4 Does he has to meet his niece at the airport?

5 We're going to the beach this weekend, but I no can swim.

6 Alex can to go out for dinner tonight.

7 She doesn't have to working late tomorrow.

   She cans go out for dinner.

8 Can he visits his in-laws next weekend?

9 You have to filling out an application for your English class.

10 Do we have to studying now? We're watching TV.

Can and have to: information questions

Can

Where **can I play** soccer around here? (Try the park.)
When **can they come** for lunch? (After class.)
How often **can we go** running? (Any time. Our afternoons are free.)
What languages **can she speak**? (She can speak Italian and Russian.)

Have to

What **does** he **have to do** tomorrow? (He has to go shopping.)
How often **does** she **have to work** late? (Not often.)
When **do** they **have to buy** the tickets? (This afternoon.)
Where **do** you **have to go** this morning? (To the airport.)

Be careful! See the difference when Who is the object or the subject.
Who **can** they **visit** on the weekend? They can visit **their cousins**. (object)
Who **do** you **have to call**? I have to call **my boss**. (object)
Who **can visit** his cousin on the weekend? **John** can. (subject)
Who **has to write** the report? **My boss** does. (subject)

B Complete the questions, using the cues and <u>can</u>.

1 A: _____ basketball around here? (Where / I / play)
   B: Try the school. It isn't far.

2 A: _____ dinner together? (When / we / have)
   B: How about tomorrow night?

3 A: I need some fresh air. _____ walking? (Where / I / go)
   B: You can go to the park. It's very nice.

4 A: _____ English? (How often / you / study)
   B: Not as much as I'd like to. I'm too busy.

5 A: _____ breakfast tomorrow morning? (Who / make)
   B: What about Bill? He always wakes up early.

6 A: _____ with about English classes? (Who / I / speak)
   B: The receptionist can help you.

C Complete the questions and answers, using <u>have to</u> or <u>has to</u>.

1 A: _____ he _____ (do) tomorrow?
   B: He _____ (go) to class.

2 A: _____ she _____ (call) the office?
   B: She _____ (call) every morning.

3 A: _____ he _____ (go) to the airport?
   B: He _____ (leave) here at 3:00.

4 A: _____ they _____ (send) the form to?
   B: They can't send it. They _____ (take) it to the office.

5 A: _____ you _____ (meet) after class?
   B: I _____ (meet) my sister. We're going to the movies.

6 A: _____ (help) the teacher after class?
   B: Chris and Tania. They _____ (clean) the board.

Can and be able to: present and past forms

You can also use <u>be able to</u> + base form for ability or possibility. <u>Can</u> is more frequent in spoken language.
I **can play** the violin. = I'm **able to play** the violin. (ability)
Bill **can meet** you at six. = Bill **is able to meet** you at six. (possibility)
They **can't call** this afternoon. = They **aren't able to call** this afternoon. (possibility)
He **can't fix** cars. = He **isn't able to fix** cars. (ability)

Use <u>could</u> or <u>was</u> / <u>were able to</u> + base form to talk about the past.
When I was four I **could swim** (or **was able to swim**).
They **could speak** (or **were able to speak**) French before they were ten.
She **couldn't be** (or **wasn't able to be**) there yesterday because she had a meeting.
We **couldn't understand** (or **weren't able to understand**) the directions.

Be careful! Use <u>was</u> / <u>were able to</u> (**NOT** <u>could</u>) for affirmative past statements of <u>possibility</u>.
She **was able to be** there yesterday. NOT She ~~could be~~ there yesterday.

D On a separate sheet of paper, change <u>can</u> to <u>be able to</u> in the following sentences.

1 She can swim very well.

2 They can't ride a bicycle.

3 George can meet you at the airport.

4 Lucy can't take the bus to the mall.

E On a separate sheet of paper, change the following statements from the present to the past.

1 We're able to help him.

2 The Martins can't go to the concert.

3 She is able to be there at seven.

4 Nicole can cook for the party.

5 Rachel and Brooke aren't able to play basketball at the school.

UNIT 6 Lesson 2

The simple present tense: non-action verbs

Some verbs are non-action verbs. Most non-action verbs are not usually used in the present continuous, even when they are describing something that is happening right now.
I **want** a sandwich. NOT I ~~am wanting~~ a sandwich.

Some non-action verbs have action and non-action meanings.

non-action meaning	action meaning
I **have** two sandwiches. (possession)	I'm **having** a sandwich. (eating)
I **think** English is easy. (opinion)	I'm **thinking** about her. (the act of thinking)

Some non-action verbs

be	miss
have	need
know	see
like	understand
love	want

A Complete the letter. Use the simple present tense or the present continuous form of the verbs.

Dear Keith,
    It's 2:00 and I _____ (1 think) of you. The kids _____
(2 play) outside. I _____ (3 see) them through the window right
now. They ___ _____ (4 have) a small table and chairs and they
_____ (5 have) a late lunch. I _____ (6 want) to send this
before I go to work. I _____ (7 know) you're working hard and we all
_____ (8 miss) you.
Maggie

The simple present tense: placement of frequency adverbs

Frequency adverbs generally go after the verb <u>be</u> and before other verbs.
I **am usually** at the pool on Saturdays.
I **usually go** to the pool on Saturdays.

<u>Sometimes</u>, <u>usually</u>, <u>often</u>, <u>generally</u>, and <u>occasionally</u> can also go at the beginning or end of a sentence.
Sometimes I go to the mall on Saturdays.
I go to the pool **occasionally**.

Be careful! Don't use <u>never</u> or <u>always</u> at the beginning or end of a sentence.
Don't say: ~~Never I go to the pool.~~ OR ~~I go to the pool always~~.

In negative sentences, most frequency adverbs can go before or after <u>don't</u> or <u>doesn't</u>.
Hank **usually doesn't** go running on the weekend.
Hank **doesn't usually** go running on the weekend.

Be careful! The frequency adverb <u>always</u> cannot go before <u>don't</u> or <u>doesn't</u>.
I **don't always** have breakfast in the morning. NOT I ~~always don't~~ have breakfast in the morning.

Be careful! Don't use <u>never</u> with a negative verb. Use the frequency adverb <u>ever</u>.
I **never eat** sweets. OR I **don't ever** eat sweets. NOT I ~~don't never~~ eat sweets.

Time expressions

Time expressions generally go at the beginning or end of a sentence. When a time expression is at the beginning, a comma is optional. Don't use a comma when the time expression is at the end.
Three times a week, I go to the pool.   I go to the pool **three times a week**.

The time expression <u>a lot</u> goes at the end of a sentence.
I go to the pool **a lot**. NOT ~~A lot I go to the pool~~.

Some time expressions
every week
every other day
once a month
twice a year
three times a week

Other expressions
once in a while
a lot

B On a separate sheet of paper, rewrite these sentences correctly.

1 She plays usually golf on Sunday.
2 They go to the park hardly ever.
3 I always am hungry in the afternoon.
4 We once in a while have eggs for breakfast.
5 Penny doesn't never exercise.

6 Never I go swimming at night.
7 Vivian doesn't drink always coffee.
8 Corey and I play twice a week tennis together.
9 We go often bike riding in the afternoon.
10 She is every day late for class.

UNIT 7 Lesson 1

The past tense of <u>be</u>: form

Use <u>was</u> and <u>were</u> for affirmative statements. Use <u>wasn't</u> and <u>weren't</u> for negative statements.
I **was** in Rome yesterday.   They **were** in Paris.
She **wasn't** on time.   They **weren't** early.

Begin <u>yes</u> / <u>no</u> questions with <u>Was</u> or <u>Were</u>.
Was your flight late?   **Were** you late?

Begin information questions with a question word followed by <u>was</u> or <u>were</u>.
How long was your vacation?   **How many** people **were** there?
Where was your passport?   **Where were** your tickets?

A Complete the conversations with <u>was</u>, <u>were</u>, <u>wasn't</u>, or <u>weren't</u>.

1 A: _____ you out of town last week?
    B: No, I _____. Why?
    A: Well, you _____ at work all week.

2 A: How _____ the food?
    B: Great! There _____ lots of fresh seafood
    and the fruit _____ delicious.

3 A: So _____ your vacation OK?
    B: Well, actually it _____. The food _____
    terrible and there _____ too many people.

4 A: Where _____ you last weekend?
    B: I _____ on vacation.
    A: Really? How _____ it?

5 A: How long _____ your trip?
    B: Only a few hours, but we _____ pretty tired.

6 A: _____ your brother on vacation last week?
    B: Yes, he _____. He and his wife _____
    on a cruise.

B On a separate sheet of paper, unscramble the words to write questions, using <u>was</u> or <u>were</u>.

1 your / vacation / very long
2 your luggage / where
3 the drive / comfortable
4 you / on the morning flight
5 your friends / late
6 there / a lot of people / on the train

UNIT 7 Lesson 2

The simple past tense: spelling rules for regular verbs

Form the past tense of most verbs by adding <u>-ed</u> to the base form.
play → play**ed**

For verbs ending in <u>-e</u> or <u>-ie</u>, add <u>-d</u>.
smile → smile**d**　　　　　　tie → tie**d**

For one-syllable verbs ending in one vowel + one consonant, double the consonant and add <u>-ed</u>.
stop → stop**ped**　　　　plan → plan**ned**

For two-syllable verbs ending in one vowel + one consonant: If the first syllable is stressed, add <u>-ed</u>.
v**i** - sit → visit**ed**

If the second syllable is stressed, double the consonant and add <u>-ed</u>.
pre - f**er** → prefer**red**

For verbs ending in a consonant and <u>-y</u>, change the <u>-y</u> to <u>-i</u> and add <u>-ed</u>.
study → stud**ied**

Be careful! Do not use <u>-ed</u> for irregular verbs.

See page 122 for a list of irregular verbs in the simple past tense form.

A On a separate sheet of paper, write the simple past tense form of the following verbs.

1 return _____
2 like _____
3 change _____
4 cry _____
5 try _____
6 stay _____
7 travel _____
8 arrive _____
9 rain _____
10 wait _____
11 offer _____
12 hurry _____

B On a separate sheet of paper, write the simple past tense form of these irregular verbs.

1 eat _____
2 drink _____
3 swim _____
4 go _____
5 write _____
6 meet _____
7 run _____
8 begin _____
9 buy _____
10 read _____
11 pay _____
12 understand _____

The simple past tense: usage and form

Use the simple past tense to talk about completed actions in the past.

My grandparents **went** to Paris in April.
Last year, we **played** tennis and **did** aerobics every day.

Negative forms
Use <u>didn't</u> + the base form of a verb.

He **didn't go** out last weekend. NOT He didn't went out last weekend.
They **didn't have** a good time. NOT They didn't had a good time.

Questions
Begin <u>yes</u> / <u>no</u> questions with <u>Did</u>. Use the base form of the verb.

Did you **go** swimming every day? NOT **Did** you went swimming every day?

Begin information questions with a question word followed by <u>did</u>. Use the base form of the verb.

Where did you **go** shopping?   **When did** he **arrive**?   **What did** they **eat** every day?

C On a separate sheet of paper, change each affirmative statement into a negative statement.

1 I slept all night.

2 We went swimming.

3 She ate a lot of food.

4 They drank a lot of coffee.

5 We had dinner at eight.

6 He bought postcards.

D On a separate sheet of paper, unscramble the words to write questions. Use the simple past tense.

1 you / go / where / on vacation last summer

2 you / from vacation / get back / when

3 they / a good flight / have

4 in London / you / do / what

5 your parents / their trip / enjoy

6 stay / how long / in Paris / Alicia

UNIT 8 Lesson 1

Direct objects: usage

The subject of a sentence performs the action of the verb. A direct object receives the action of the verb.

subject	verb	direct object
I	like	**spicy food**.
Anne	wears	**dark clothes**.

A Underline the subjects in the following sentences. Circle the direct objects.

1 <u>Stacey</u> is wearing (a bathrobe) right now.

2 Many people buy outerwear in this store.

3 I love red shoes.

4 Sanford and Gloria never wear shorts.

5 You can't enter this store before 10:00.

6 Do you have your credit card?

7 Marianne wants a pair of warm pajamas.

Indirect objects: usage rules and common errors

When a sentence contains a direct object and a prepositional phrase, you can use an indirect object to say the same thing.

prepositional phrase	indirect object
I'm buying the gloves **for her**.	I'm buying **her** the gloves.
Give the sweater **to Jay**.	Give **Jay** the sweater.

Be careful! When a sentence contains both a direct object and an indirect object, the indirect object always comes first. The direct object CANNOT be a pronoun.

Mindy wrote **her parents a letter**.   NOT Mindy wrote a letter her parents.   NOT Mindy wrote her parents it.
Mindy wrote **them a letter**.   NOT Mindy wrote a letter them.   NOT Mindy wrote them it.

B On a separate sheet of paper, rewrite each sentence, changing the prepositional phrase into an indirect object pronoun. Follow the example.

> She buys clothes for them. *She buys them clothes.*

1 Laurie sends a check to her father every month. **3** They serve meals to us in the dining room.

2 At night we read stories to our children. **4** They never give gifts to me on my birthday.

C On a separate sheet of paper, rewrite each sentence, changing the indirect object pronoun into a prepositional phrase using the preposition in parentheses. Follow the example.

> They never buy me dinner. (for) *They never buy dinner for me.*

1 He always gives me the check. (to) **3** His friend showed him the check for dinner. (to)

2 I sent my colleagues the tickets. (to) **4** She'd like to get her mother a book. (for)

D On a separate sheet of paper, rewrite the following sentences, adding the indirect object or prepositional phrase to each sentence. Don't add any words. Follow the example.

> They sent it on Monday. (to me) *They sent it to me on Monday.*

1 Did they give breakfast at the hotel? (you) **3** They make lunch every day. (for him)

2 We always tell the truth. (her) **4** He brought flowers last night. (his wife)

UNIT 8   *Lesson 2*

Comparative adjectives: spelling rules

Add -er to one-syllable adjectives. If the adjective ends in -e, add -r.
tight → tighter   loose → looser

If an adjective ends in a consonant-vowel-consonant sequence, double the final consonant before adding -er.
hot → hotter

For most adjectives that end in -y, change the y to i and add -er.
pretty → prettier   busy → busier

To make the comparative form of most adjectives that have more than two syllables, use more or less.
affordable → more affordable   convenient → less convenient

When comparing two things that are both in the sentence, use than before the second thing.
She's less practical **than** her sister.   The weather is warmer there **than** here.

A On a separate sheet of paper, write the comparative form of the following adjectives.

1 tall	**5** light	**9** sad	**13** spicy	**17** popular
2 sunny	**6** clean	**10** fatty	**14** healthy	**18** red
3 comfortable	**7** bad	**11** salty	**15** cute	**19** conservative
4 heavy	**8** late	**12** sweet	**16** short	**20** interesting

B Complete each sentence with a comparative adjective. Use **than** if necessary.

1 I like the pink purse. It's much _____ (nice).

2 Low-fat milk is not bad, but no-fat milk is _____ (good).

3 France is _____ (small) Russia.

4 Women's shoes are usually _____ (expensive) men's shoes.

5 It's hot during the day, but it's _____ (cool) at night.

6 He's a lot _____ (tall) his brother.

7 This projector is a lot _____ (popular), but it's _____ (affordable).

8 They're much _____ (liberal) about clothing rules at the beach.

9 It's usually _____ (sunny) in the morning before the rain begins.

10 French fries are _____ (fatty) and _____ (salty) a salad.

Modals *can*, *could*, and *should*: meaning, form, and common errors

Meaning
Use <u>can</u> to express ability or possibility.
Jerome **can** speak Korean.   I **can** be there before 8:00.

Use <u>could</u> to suggest an alternative or to make a weak suggestion.
They **could** see an old movie like *Titanic*, or they **could** go to something new.
You **could** eat a healthier diet.

Use <u>should</u> to give advice or to express criticism.
You **should** think before you speak.

Form
Modals are followed by the base form of the main verb of the sentence, except in short answers to questions.
You **can eat** at a lot of good restaurants in this neighborhood.
Who should read this? They **should**.
Can you see the moon tonight? Yes, I **can**.

Use <u>not</u> between the modal and the base form.
You **shouldn't** stay at the Galaxy Hotel.   They **can't** take the express.

In <u>yes</u> / <u>no</u> questions, the modal precedes the subject of the sentence. In information questions, the question word precedes the modal.

Yes / no questions	Information questions
Should I buy a round-trip ticket?	When **should** they leave?
Can we make the 1:05 flight?	Why **should** they go?
Could she take an express train?	Which trains **could** I take?
	Who **could** they call?

> **BUT:** Note the word order when <u>Who</u> is the subject.
> **Who can give** me the information?
> (The travel agent can.)

Common errors
Never add <u>-s</u> to the third-person singular form of modals.
He **should buy** a ticket in advance. NOT ~~He shoulds buy~~ a ticket in advance.

Never use <u>to</u> between modals and the base form.
You **could take** the train or the bus. NOT You ~~could to take~~ the train or the bus.

Circle the correct phrases to complete the sentences.

1 Who (should buy / should to buy) the tickets?

2 Where (I can find / can I find) a hotel?

3 You (could to walk / could walk) or (take / taking) the bus.

4 (I should to call / Should I call) you when I arrive?

5 We (can to not take / can't take) the bus; it left.

6 When (should you giving / should you give) the agent your boarding pass?

7 Which trains (can get / can getting) me there soon?

Expansion: future actions

There are four ways to express future actions, using present forms.

Be going to
<u>Be going to</u> + base form usually expresses a future plan or certain knowledge about the future.
I'm **going to spend** my summer in Africa.   She's **going to** get a rental car when she arrives.
It's **going to** rain tomorrow.

The present continuous
The present continuous can also express a future plan.
We're **traveling** tonight.   We **aren't wearing** formal clothes to the wedding.
We **aren't eating** at home tomorrow.

The simple present tense

The simple present tense can express a future action, especially with verbs of motion: <u>arrive</u>, <u>come</u>, <u>depart</u>, <u>fly</u>, <u>go</u>, <u>leave</u>, <u>sail</u>, and <u>start</u>—especially when on a schedule or a timetable. When the simple present tense expresses the future, there is almost always a word, phrase, or clause indicating the future time.

This Monday, the express **leaves** at noon.   The flight **arrives** at 9:00 tonight.

The present of <u>be</u>

The present of <u>be</u> can describe a future event if it includes a word or phrase that indicates the future.

The wedding **is** on Sunday.

A Read the arrival and departure schedules. Then complete each sentence or question with the simple present tense.

1 The bus _____ at 11:00. It _____ at 8:00.

2 When _____ the flight _____?
It _____ at 23:30.

3 What time _____ the train _____
in Beijing? At 10:20 P.M.

4 _____ the train _____ at 7:00? Yes, it does.

B On a separate sheet of paper, answer each of the following questions with a complete sentence. There may be more than one correct way to answer each question.

1 What are your plans for your next vacation?

2 What are you going to do this weekend?

3 What are you doing this evening?

UNIT 10 *Lesson 1*

Comparative and superlative adjectives: usage and form

Usage

Comparative adjectives compare two people, places, or things. Use <u>than</u> if the second item is mentioned right after the adjective.

Mexico City is **larger than** Los Angeles.   Housing in New York is **more expensive than** in Lima.

Compared with Los Angeles, Mexico City is **larger**.   Compared with Lima, housing is **more expensive** in New York.

Superlative adjectives compare more than two people, places, or things.

Compared to other cities in the Americas, Mexico City is **the largest**.

> **Be careful!** Use <u>the</u> with superlative adjectives.
> Don't say: Mexico City is ~~largest~~.

Form

adjective	comparative adjective	superlative adjective
cheap	**cheaper (than)**	**the cheapest**
expensive	**more expensive (than)**	**the most expensive**
practical	**less practical (than)**	**the least practical**

Superlative adjectives: spelling

Add **-est** to one-syllable adjectives. If the adjective ends in **-e**, add **-st**.

cheap → the cheap**est**   loose → the loos**est**

If an adjective ends in a consonant-vowel-consonant sequence, double the final consonant before adding **-est**.

hot → the hot**test**

For most adjectives that end in **-y**, change the y to **i** and add **-est**.

pretty → the prett**iest**   busy → the bus**iest**

To form the superlative of most adjectives of two or more syllables, use **the most** or **the least**.

Car trips are **the least expensive** vacations.   Cruises are **the most relaxing** vacations.

A Write <u>both</u> the comparative and superlative form of each of the following adjectives.

	comparative	superlative			comparative	superlative
1 tall	_____	_____		**10** interesting	_____	_____
2 easy	_____	_____		**11** conservative	_____	_____
3 liberal	_____	_____		**12** light	_____	_____
4 heavy	_____	_____		**13** casual	_____	_____
5 unusual	_____	_____		**14** comfortable	_____	_____
6 pretty	_____	_____		**15** relaxing	_____	_____
7 exciting	_____	_____		**16** long	_____	_____
8 wild	_____	_____		**17** short	_____	_____
9 informal	_____	_____		**18** scary	_____	_____

B Complete each sentence with a comparative or superlative adjective. Use <u>than</u> if necessary.

1 That dinner was _____ (delicious) meal we had on our vacation.

2 This scanner is definitely _____ (good) other one.

3 The Caribbean cruise is _____ (relaxing) of our vacation packages.

4 The Honsu X24 is a good camera, but the Cashio is _____ (easy) to use.

5 We have several brands, but I'd say the R300 is _____ (popular).

6 Sunday was _____ (bad) day of our vacation.

7 I like that rug, but I think this one is _____ (beautiful).

8 Our vacation in Brazil was _____ (nice) our vacation in Italy last year.

9 There are so many brands to choose from. Which brand is _____ (good)?

10 All three cameras look good. But which one is _____ (easy) to use?

11 I like both the J12 and the Pro MP3 players, but which one's _____ (small)?

12 Which of these three plates do you think is _____ (pretty)?

13 I can't decide if I should read this book or that one. Which one is _____ (interesting)?

UNIT 10 *Lesson 2*

Intensifiers <u>very</u>, <u>really</u>, and <u>too</u>

Intensifiers make the meaning of adjectives stronger.

<u>Very</u> and <u>really</u> have the same meaning. They can intensify adjectives with a positive or negative meaning.
> That restaurant is **really** (or **very**) **good**. I want to go there.
> That movie is **really** (or **very**) **scary**. I don't want to see it.

<u>Too</u> also makes the meaning of adjectives stronger. But <u>too</u> expresses the idea of "more than enough." <u>Too</u> usually has a negative meaning.
> That movie is **too long**. I don't want to see it.
> This restaurant is **too expensive**. I'm not going to eat here.

Be careful! Don't use <u>too</u> to intensify adjectives with a positive meaning. Use <u>very</u> and <u>really</u>.
> This camera is **very** affordable! NOT This camera is ~~too affordable~~!

A **Complete each sentence with too, really, or very and your own adjective.**

1 Beach vacations are _____. I love them.

2 French fries are _____. You shouldn't eat them every day.

3 A cruise is _____. I don't have enough money to take one.

4 They say this movie is _____. I want to see it.

5 This book is _____. You should read it.

6 English is _____. People are learning it all over the world.

7 This printer is _____. I need to replace it.

8 These pants are _____. I need to buy a larger pair.

B **Complete each conversation, using too or enough.**

1 A: How about this? Should we buy it for your mother?
   B: No. It isn't _____ (pretty). I want something nicer.

2 A: Do you think this rug is too small?
   B: No, it's great. I think it's _____ (big).

3 A: Did you buy a microwave yesterday?
   B: I looked at some. But they were _____ (expensive).

4 A: Why are you sending that steak back to the chef?
   B: It's an expensive meal, and this steak just isn't _____ (good).

5 A: You never eat dessert?
   B: No. Desserts are _____ (sweet) for me.

6 A: How was your vacation?
   B: To tell the truth, it just wasn't _____ (relaxing).

7 A: How's that soup? Is it _____ (hot)?
   B: No, it's fine. Thanks.

8 A: Would you like more ice in your water?
   B: Yes, please. It isn't _____ (cold).

Writing Booster

The Writing Booster is optional. It is intended to teach students the conventions of written English. Each unit's Writing Booster is focused both on a skill and its application to the Writing Exercise from the Unit Review page.

UNIT 1 *Capitalization*

Use a capital letter to begin a sentence.
It's a pleasure to introduce my classmate.

Use a capital letter for:

cities / countries	I live in Beijing. He's from Colombia.
nationalities	They're Honduran.
languages	I speak Russian and Italian.
days and months	My birthday is on Tuesday, June 19th.
the word I	My brother and I are students.
formal titles and names	I'd like you to meet Mr. Smith.

A On a separate sheet of paper, rewrite each sentence, using correct capitalization.

1 please say hello to julio cueva from peru.

2 my friend mr. lee is a computer programmer from korea.

3 he is brazilian, and his birthday is in october.

4 my classmate ms. silva is twenty-six years old.

5 miss wang teaches chinese to college students.

6 this monday john met his friend mr. abe.

7 when i travel, i need to use english.

B Guidance for Writing (page 12) Ask a classmate the questions below. Use the answers as a guide for your writing. Add more information if you can. Make sure you use capital letters correctly.

- What's your partner's name?
- Does your partner have a nickname?
- How old is your partner?
- What's your partner's occupation?
- What is your partner's hometown?
- Is your partner's hometown his or her birthplace?
- What's your partner's favorite actor?
- What's your partner's favorite sport?

UNIT 2 *The sentence*

In English, a sentence is a group of words that expresses a thought. A sentence has a subject and a verb. When you write a sentence, begin with a capital letter and end with a period.

subject	verb	subject	verb
The play	is great.	She	loves music.

A Circle the subject and underline the verb in each sentence.

1 Her children like folk music.

2 I prefer CDs to cassettes.

3 My boyfriend loves classical music.

4 Their favorite musician is Beck.

5 The play isn't very good.

B Write an X next to the words or groups of words that are not sentences.

☐ 1 A theater fan.

☐ 2 The theater is down the street from the park.

☐ 3 And around the corner from the art gallery.

☐ 4 I listen to music in the shower.

☐ 5 Really loud concerts.

☐ 6 Downloading music.

Ideas
- your favorite music
- your favorite artist
- when you listen to music
- where you buy music
- how many CDs you own

C Guidance for Writing (page 24) Use the ideas as a guide to help you write five sentences about your musical tastes. Begin each sentence with a capital letter and end each sentence with a period. Be sure to use a subject and a verb in each sentence.

And

Use <u>and</u> to combine two sentences if you want to add information. It's common, but not necessary, to use a comma before <u>and</u>.

My cousin loves rock music, **and** she's a great dancer.

But

Use <u>but</u> to combine two sentences if you want to show a difference or contrast. It's common, but not necessary, to use a comma before <u>but</u>.

My cousin loves rock music, **but** I love classical.
My cousin loves rock music, **but** I don't.

Be careful! In traditional formal writing, writers avoid beginning sentences with <u>And</u> or <u>But</u>.

Don't write: My cousin loves rock music. ~~And she's a great dancer.~~
Don't write: My cousin loves rock music. ~~But I don't.~~

A **On a separate sheet of paper, combine these sentences, using <u>and</u>.**

1 My sister-in-law has long hair. She's very pretty.

2 My aunt is a computer programmer. Her husband is a teacher.

3 We look alike. We wear the same clothes.

4 My cousin likes classical music. He loves Italian food.

5 We look completely different. We like different kinds of music.

B **On a separate sheet of paper, combine these sentences, using <u>but</u>.**

1 My brother wears old clothes. I wear new clothes.

2 My sister has long hair. I have short hair.

3 My cousin lives near the airport. His parents don't.

4 I love rock music. My stepfather doesn't.

5 We look alike. We wear completely different clothes.

C **Guidance for Writing (page 36) Use the ideas to help you write six statements comparing two people in your family. Use <u>and</u> or <u>but</u> to combine sentences.**

Ideas
- appearance
- musical tastes
- food preferences
- clothing preferences
- birthplaces and hometowns
- marital status
- favorite colors

And

Remember that <u>and</u> connects two sentences and makes them one sentence.

I like fruit, **and** I also like vegetables.

You can also use <u>and</u> to connect words in a series. Notice the use of the comma in the examples below.

I like apples, oranges, grapes, **and** other fruits.

Be careful! Don't use a comma when <u>and</u> connects only two words.

I like apples and oranges. NOT ~~I like apples, and oranges.~~

In addition

<u>In addition</u> connects the ideas in one sentence with the ideas in the next sentence. Use a comma after <u>in addition</u>.

I like fruit. **In addition,** I like vegetables.
I like apples and oranges. **In addition,** I like grapes and other fruits.

A **Connect the following words and ideas with <u>and</u> or <u>in addition</u>.**

1 The people eat a lot of vegetables in Spain, Italy, _____ France.

2 In the U.S., many restaurants serve big portions. _____ , there are a lot of fatty foods.

3 There are five or six great Italian restaurants near the hotel. _____ , there are two restaurants where the menu has dishes from Mexico, Thailand, India, _____ even Indonesia!

4 She loves pasta, _____ I want to invite her to my favorite Italian restaurant.

5 Raw carrots taste great, _____ they're good for you.

6 This restaurant has great food. _____ , the service is excellent.

7 You can choose from six entrées on the menu, _____ they all come with a choice of vegetable.

8 I usually order soup, salad, a main course, _____ dessert.

B **Guidance for Writing (page 48)** Read the description of food in the United States. Use these paragraphs as a guide to help you write about the food of your country. Change the details so the sentences describe your food.

American food is more than hamburgers, hot dogs, and pancakes. The best American food is regional. One regional specialty is clam chowder. Clam chowder is a delicious soup from the northeast coast. In Boston, clam chowder contains milk, and in New York it contains tomatoes. Clam chowder always contains Atlantic clams. In addition, clam chowder always contains some vegetables, such as onions, potatoes, peppers, or corn.

Another famous regional specialty of American cooking is barbecue. Barbecue comes from the center and south of the United States. Barbecue style is not always the same, but it always has meat and a spicy sauce. Americans are very proud of barbecue. Many restaurants claim that they have the only authentic barbecue. When you travel to the United States, be sure to try some regional specialties like clam chowder and barbecue.

UNIT 5 *Placement of adjectives: before nouns and after the verb <u>be</u>*

Adjectives are words that describe nouns and pronouns.
noun   pronoun
The old **photocopier** is obsolete. **It's** also broken.

Adjectives come before nouns or after the verb <u>be</u> when the subject of a sentence is a noun or pronoun.
I have a **new computer**.
The computer **is new**. **It's terrific**.

Be careful! Adjectives don't come after nouns. Adjectives don't have plural forms.
new refrigerators
NOT ~~refrigerators new~~
NOT ~~news refrigerators~~

When two adjectives describe the same noun, connect them with <u>and</u>. When there are more than two, use commas.
The microwave is **popular** and **convenient**.
This camera is **obsolete, broken**, and **defective**.

Adjectives
broken
obsolete
defective
terrible
awful
great
terrific
awesome

fast
popular
guaranteed
affordable
convenient
good
fixable

Some adjectives are compound phrases.
This scanner is really **up-to-date**.
She bought an **out-of-date** camcorder.

A **Circle the adjectives in each sentence.**

1 My old printer is obsolete.

2 This MP3 is very convenient. And it's portable, too.

3 Is your scanner fixable?

4 This terrible car is a lemon! It's awful.

5 Our new washing machine is both good and guaranteed.

B **On a separate sheet of paper, write sentences about five of the following products. Use the adjectives from the chart above.**

Products
a smart phone   a digital camera
a mobile / cell phone   a TV
a GPS   a camcorder
a laptop (computer)   A DVD player
a desktop (computer)

Smart phones are very convenient.

C Guidance for Writing (page 60) Use your answers to the following questions as a guide to help you write a paragraph about a product you use.

- What is it?
- What brand is it?
- What model is it?
- Is it a good product? Why or why not?
- What does it do?

- What adjectives describe it?
- Where do you use it?
- Is it working?
- Does it drive you crazy?
- How old is it?

UNIT 6 *Punctuation of statements and questions*

. (a period)
? (a question mark)
! (an exclamation point)
, (a comma)

Remember:
Use commas to connect more than two ideas in a series.
I go to the gym, run in the park, and go bike riding every weekend.

Use a period at the end of a statement.
I go to the gym every morning.

Use a question mark at the end of a question.
What do you do to stay in shape?

Use an exclamation point at the end of a sentence if you want to indicate that something is funny or surprising.
The truth is I'm a couch potato!

A Rewrite each statement or question, using correct punctuation. Remember to begin each with a capital letter.

1 she doesn't have time to exercise
2 do you get enough sleep every night
3 my friends think I exercise a lot but I don't
4 we go running bike riding and swimming in the summer

5 my father never eats sweets
6 what do you do on weekends
7 they eat junk food watch TV and stay up late every night
8 are you a couch potato

B Guidance for Writing (page 72) Use the ideas as a guide to help you write six questions about fitness and eating habits for your interview.

Ideas
- favorite activities
- exercise routines
- foods you eat
- foods you avoid
- what you can or can't do

UNIT 7 *Time order*

Use a time clause in a sentence to show the order of events.
We visited the old part of town **after we had lunch**.
We checked into our hotel **before we had lunch**.

You can begin a sentence with a time clause. Most writers use a comma when the time clause comes first.
After we had lunch, we visited the old part of town.
Before we had lunch, we checked into our hotel

Use transition signals to show time order in a paragraph. Use <u>First</u> to begin a series and <u>Finally</u> to end one. Use <u>Then</u>, <u>Next</u>, and <u>After that</u> to indicate a series of events. Commas are optional.
   First, we checked in to our hotel. **After** we had lunch, we visited the old part of town and took pictures. **Then,** we went to the beach and lay in the sun for a while. **Next,** we played golf. **After that,** we went shopping and bought a rug. **Finally,** we went back to our hotel.

A On a separate sheet of paper, use the cues to write sentences. Begin each sentence with a time clause. Follow the example.

(before) First we had lunch. Then we went to the beach.   *Before we went to the beach, we had lunch.*

1 (after) First we visited Rome. Then we went to Venice.
2 (before) First they went snorkeling. After that, they had lunch.
3 (after) He arrived in Miami on Saturday. Then he looked for a hotel.

4 (before) I spent three days in Mexico City. Next I flew to Cancún.
5 (after) She got back from the airport. After that, she called her mother.
6 (before) The weather was beautiful. Then it rained.

B On a separate sheet of paper, rewrite the paragraph, using time-order transition words.

> Let me tell you about my trip. I flew from New York to London. It was very interesting, and I spent two days there. I took the train through the Chunnel to Paris. Paris was amazing. I got a car and drove to Rome. It was a long drive, but it was really scenic. I took a boat to the island of Sardinia. It was very beautiful. I flew back to London and back home to New York.

C Guidance for Writing (page 84) Write sentences describing your vacation in the order that the events happened. Then use them to write your paragraph, using time clauses and time-order transition words.

UNIT 8 *Connecting ideas with <u>because</u> and <u>since</u>*

Clauses with <u>because</u> and <u>since</u> present reasons. There's no difference in meaning between <u>because</u> and <u>since</u> in the following sentences.
> I'm going to Paris **because I love French food.**
> He's not wearing a jacket **since he left it in the restaurant.**

In speaking, it's OK to answer a question using just a clause with <u>because</u> or <u>since</u>.
> A: Why are you wearing jeans?
> B: **Because it's a really casual restaurant.**

In writing, however, a clause beginning with <u>because</u> or <u>since</u> is not a sentence; it's an incomplete thought. Connect the clause beginning with <u>because</u> or <u>since</u> to a sentence to make the thought complete.
> **I wear jeans at that restaurant** because it is a really casual restaurant.

A clause with <u>because</u> or <u>since</u> can come at the beginning or the end of the sentence. When it comes at the beginning, use a comma. It's good writing style to vary placement so all sentences don't sound the same.
> I eat vegetables every day **because they are healthy.**
> **Because they are healthy,** I eat vegetables every day.

Remember:
In English, a sentence is a group of words containing a subject and a verb. It expresses a complete thought.

A On a separate sheet of paper, connect the sentences, using clauses with either <u>because</u> or <u>since</u>. Be careful! make sure the clause with <u>because</u> or <u>since</u> presents a reason.

1 I'm wearing a sweater. I feel cold.

2 She called her brother. It was his birthday.

3 He bought a blue blazer. He needed it for a business trip.

4 They didn't have a ticket for the concert. They stayed home.

5 Our DVD player is broken. We have to get a new one.

B On a separate sheet of paper, answer each of the following questions with a complete sentence containing a clause with <u>because</u> or <u>since</u>. Follow the example.

Why do you like dance music?   *I like dance music because it is happy music.*

1 Why are you studying English?

2 Why is a clothes store better than a clothes website?

3 Why do people like malls?

4 Why are running shoes more comfortable than formal shoes?

C Guidance for Writing (page 96) Write a list of at least five clothing do's and don'ts for appropriate dress in your country. Explain the reasons for the tips, using <u>because</u> and <u>since</u>. Use your sentences as a guide to help you write your letter or e-mail.

> *Don't wear jeans to nice restaurants because people think they're inappropriate.*

A paragraph is a group of sentences that relate to a topic or a theme. When your writing contains information about a variety of topics, it is convenient to divide your writing into separate paragraphs.

Traditionally, **the first word of a paragraph is indented**. (Sometimes new paragraphs, especially in books, are not indented. Instead, a separation is made by leaving a blank line space as below.)

In the writing model to the right, the first paragraph is about Holland and the second is about Thailand. Dividing the writing into two paragraphs makes it easier to read and understand.

Clothing customs in different countries

Holland has a northern climate, so depending on the time of year you're visiting, pack lighter or heavier clothes. One thing people notice about Holland is the way young people dress. Their dress code is "anything goes," so it's not unusual to see some pretty wild clothes there.

On the other hand, if you're visiting Thailand from May to September, pack for the heat. Thailand is generally conservative when it comes to clothing, but at Thailand's magnificent temples, the rules about clothing, and especially shoes, are very strict. If your shoes are too open, they are considered disrespectful, and you will have to change to more modest ones. So be prepared with light but modest clothing and shoes for your Thailand trip.

A Write a check mark ✔ in the place or places where a new paragraph could or should start. Then, on a separate sheet of paper, copy the paragraphs, indenting each one.

Famous families

Jackie Chan is a movie star and singer from Hong Kong. His wife, Joan Lin, is an actress from Taiwan. They have a son, JC Chan. He's a student in the United States. Another famous family is the Williams family. Venus and Serena Williams are famous tennis players. Their mother's name is Oracene Price. Their father, Richard Williams, is their manager. Still another famous family is the Fernández family from Mexico. Vicente and Alejandro are father and son. They are both singers, and they are famous all over Latin America.

B Guidance for Writing (page 108) Use your answers to the questions below as a guide to help you write your paragraphs.

Paragraph 1

Begin your paragraph with an opening statement, such as: Last month, I went to ___ .

- Where did you go?
- What kind of transportation did you take?
- When did you leave?
- Who did you travel with?
- What did you do when you were there?
- When did you get back?

Paragraph 2

Begin your next paragraph with an opening statement, such as: On my next trip, ...

- Where are you going to go?
- What kind of transportation are you going to take?
- When are you leaving?
- Who are you traveling with?
- What are you going to do when you are there?
- When are you getting back?

Use <u>even though</u> to connect contradictory ideas in a sentence. (A comma is optional before <u>even though</u> when it comes at the end of the sentence.)

Bee Flowers is the most popular shop in town **even though it's quite expensive.**

You can bargain for really low prices at Marty's**, even though the service isn't very friendly.**

Always use a comma if the clause that begins with <u>even though</u> comes first.

Even though it's quite expensive, Bee Flowers is the most popular shop in town.

Even though the service isn't very friendly, you can bargain for really low prices at Marty's.

Use <u>however</u> and <u>on the other hand</u> at the beginning of a sentence to connect contradictory ideas from one sentence to another. Use a comma.

You can bargain for really low prices at Marty's. **However,** the service isn't very friendly.

Bee Flowers is quite expensive. **On the other hand,** it's the most popular shop in town.

Be careful! Don't use <u>however</u> or <u>on the other hand</u> to combine clauses in a sentence.

Don't write: You can bargain for really low prices at Marty's, ~~however the service isn't very friendly.~~

A On a separate sheet of paper, combine each pair of sentences into one sentence, using <u>even though</u>. Then rewrite your sentences, using <u>even though</u> to begin each one.

1 You can find some good deals at the Savoy Hotel. Their rooms are the most expensive in town.

2 You can bargain for really low prices at the Old Market. It isn't the prettiest place to shop.

3 The Philcov X30 is easy to use and not too expensive. It isn't the most popular camera.

4 The prices of flat screen TVs are getting lower every year. They can still be very expensive.

5 The Samson camcorder is the most professional camera you can buy. It isn't the lightest.

B Now, on a separate sheet of paper, write the sentences again, using <u>however</u> or <u>on the other hand</u>.

C Guidance for Writing (page 120) Write at least six sentences about places to shop in your town or city. Use <u>even though</u>, <u>however</u>, and <u>on the other hand</u>. Use your sentences as a guide to help you write your guide.

Top Notch Pop Lyrics

1:15/1:16

🔊))) It's Nice To Meet You   [Unit 1]

(CHORUS)
It's nice to meet you.
Good to meet you.
Pleasure to meet you.

What's your name?
My name is Mr. Johnson.
Please just call me Stan.
I'd like you to meet my wife, Mary Anne.

(CHORUS)

What do you do?
Actually, I'm a teacher
at the Children's Institute.
The little kids are really cute.
That sounds nice. Where are you from—
somewhere far or near?
As a matter of fact, Chicago is my
hometown.
Could you say that louder please?
How did you end up here?
My father was a salesman.
We moved all around.

(CHORUS)

Who is that?
Let me introduce you
to my new friend Eileen.
She's a chef and she's nineteen.

(CHORUS)

Good-bye. Take care.

1:34/1:35

🔊))) Going Out   [Unit 2]

Do you want to see a play?
What time does the play begin?
It starts at eight. Is that OK?
I'd love to go. I'll see you then.
I heard it got some good reviews.
Where's it playing? What's the show?
It's called "One Single Life to Lose."
I'll think about it. I don't know.

(CHORUS)
Everything will be all right
when you and I go out tonight.

When Thomas Soben gives his talk—
The famous chef? That's not for me!
The doors open at nine o'clock.
There's a movie we could see
at Smith and Second Avenue.
That's my favorite neighborhood!
I can't wait to be with you.
I can't wait to have some food.

(CHORUS)

We're going to have a good time.
Don't keep me up past my bedtime.
We'll make a date.
Tonight's the night.
It starts at eight.
The price is right!
I'm a fan of rock 'n' roll.

Classical is more my style.
I like blues and I like soul.
Bach and Mozart make me smile!
Around the corner and down the street.
That's the entrance to the park.
There's a place where we could meet.
I wouldn't go there after dark!

(CHORUS: 2 times)

2:18/2:19

🔊))) An Only Child   [Unit 3]

Let me see the photos of
your wife and family.
Who's that guy there, on the right,
next to the TV?
Is that your younger brother, John?
And who are those two?
Your sisters both look so alike.
Please tell me what they do.

(CHORUS)
I ask so many questions.
You just answer with a smile.
You have a large family,
but I am an only child.

How about your cousins now?
Please tell me something new.
Do they both play basketball?
You know that I do, too.

(CHORUS)

I don't have a brother,
but you have two or three.
You're all one big happy family.
I don't have a sister,
but you have older twins.
This is a game I can't ever win.
Do you have nieces and nephews,
and how many are there now?
Do they all like the same kinds of things?
Are they different somehow?

(CHORUS)

2:34/2:35

🔊))) The World Café   [Unit 4]

Is there something that you want?
Is there anything you need?
Have you made up your mind
what you want to eat?
Place your order now,
or do you need more time?
Why not start with some juice—
lemon, orange, or lime?
Some like it hot, some like it sweet,
some like it really spicy.
You may not like everything you eat,
but I think we're doing nicely.

(CHORUS)
I can understand every word you say.
Tonight we're speaking English at
The World Café.

I'll take the main course now.
I think I'll have the fish.

Does it come with the choice of another
dish?
Excuse me waiter, please—
I think I'm in the mood
for a little dessert, and the cake looks good.
Do you know? Are there any low-fat desserts
that we could try now?
I feel like having a bowl of fruit.
Do you have to say good-bye now?

(CHORUS)

Apples, oranges, cheese, and ham,
coffee, juice, milk, bread, and jam,
rice and beans, meat and potatoes,
eggs and ice cream,
grilled tomatoes—
That's the menu.
That's the list.
Is there anything I missed?

(CHORUS)

3:22/3:23

🔊))) It's Not Working Again   [Unit 5]

Hi. I'm calling on my cell phone.
I need a little help with a fax machine.
It's not working, and it's pretty bad.
I feel like I've been had, if you know
what I mean.
I'm coming to the store right now.
Can you show me how to use it?
The front lid won't open.
When my cat's around,
it squeaks and makes a funny sound.

(CHORUS)
It's not working again.
It's driving me crazy.
It's not working again.

I called yesterday, and a guy named Jack
said,
"I'm busy right now, can I call you back?"
He didn't even ask me what was wrong
with it.
He didn't want to hear the short and
long of it.
I just bought the thing yesterday,
and it won't turn on so please don't say,
"I'm sorry to hear that.
That's a shame.
That's too bad."
It's all a game.

(CHORUS)

I'm not looking for a laptop computer
or an X340 or a PDA.
Just tell me what's wrong with my fax
machine
so I can say good-bye and be on my way.
It won't send a copy of my document.
The paper goes through, and it comes
out bent.
On second thought, it's guaranteed.
I want my money back—that's what I need.

(CHORUS: 2 times)

🔊 A Typical Day [Unit 6]

The Couch Potato sits around.
He eats junk food by the pound.
It's just a typical day.
Watching as the world goes by,
he's out of shape and wonders why.
It's just a typical day.

(CHORUS)
Every night he dreams that he's
skydiving through the air.
And sometimes you appear.
He says, "What are you doing here?"

He cleans the house and plays guitar,
takes a shower, drives the car.
It's just a typical day.
He watches TV all alone,
reads and sleeps, talks on the phone.
It's just a typical day.

(CHORUS)

I'm sorry.
Mr. Couch Potato's resting right now.
Can he call you back?
He usually lies down every day of the week,
and he always has to have a snack.
Now all his dreams are coming true.
He's making plans to be with you.
It's just a typical day.
He goes dancing once a week.
He's at the theater as we speak!
It's just a typical day.

(CHORUS)

🔊 My Dream Vacation [Unit 7]

The ride was bumpy
and much too long.
It was pretty boring.
It felt so wrong.
I slept all night,
and it rained all day.
We left the road,
and we lost the way.
Then you came along
and you took my hand.
You whispered words
I could understand.

(CHORUS)
On my dream vacation,
I dream of you.
I don't ever want to wake up.
On my dream vacation,
this much is true:
I don't ever want it to stop.

The food was awful.
They stole my purse.
The whole two weeks went
from bad to worse.
They canceled my ticket.
I missed my flight.
They were so unfriendly
it just wasn't right.
So I called a taxi,
and I got inside,

and there you were,
sitting by my side.

(CHORUS)

You were so unusual.
The day was so exciting.
I opened up my eyes,
and you were gone.
I waited for hours.
You never called.
I watched TV
and looked at the walls.
Where did you go to?
Why weren't you near?
Did you have a reason
to disappear?
So I flew a plane
to the south of France,
and I heard you say,
Would you like to dance?"

(CHORUS)

🔊 Anything Goes [Unit 8]

The shoe department's upstairs.
It's on the second floor.
Women's Casual is down the stairs,
there by the door.
This helpful store directory
shows every kind of clothes.
I look for the department where
it says anything goes.

(CHORUS)
At home and when I travel,
I always like to wear
pajamas in the daytime
with a blazer and a pair
of socks on my fingers
and gloves on my toes—
anything goes.

On the ground floor, there's a restaurant
and a photo studio,
so I take the escalator
down to the floor below.
There are turtlenecks and T-shirts.
There are cardigans and jeans
in every size and color.
They look comfortable and clean.

(CHORUS)

The salesperson says,
"Here you go.
Try it on.
That's not too bad.
Let me see if I can find you something
better."
Some people say that black clothes
are more flattering than white,
or they think that they look nicer
in the day or in the night.
Their clothes can't be too liberal
or too conservative.
If I love it, then I wear it.
That's the way I want to live.

(CHORUS)

🔊 Five Hundred Ways [Unit 9]

You could take the bus,
or you could take the train.
You could take the ferry,
or you could take a plane.
Baby, it's a small world,
when all is said and done.
We have so many options,
the question is, which one?

(CHORUS)
There are five hundred ways to get here.
What are you going to do?
You could get a one-way ticket to see me.
I'm waiting here for you.

You should really hurry.
When are you going to call
and make your reservation?
You could miss them all.
And do you know how long
you are going to stay?
You could come and be with me
forever and a day.

(CHORUS)

Follow me.
Follow me.
Yes, you can follow me.
You have my phone number,
and you have my address.
Tell me, are you coming on
the local or express?

(CHORUS)

🔊 Shopping for Souvenirs [Unit 10]

I go to the bank at a quarter to ten.
I pick up my cash from the ATM.
Here at the store, it won't be too hard
to take out a check or a credit card.
The bank has a good rate of exchange,
and everything here is in my price range.
The easiest part of this bargain hunt
is that I can afford anything I want.

(CHORUS)
Whenever I travel around the world,
I spend my money for two.
Shopping for souvenirs
helps me to be near you.

I try to decide how much I should pay
for the beautiful art I see on display.
To get a great deal, I can't be too nice.
It can't hurt to ask for a better price.

(CHORUS)

Yes, it's gorgeous, and I love it.
It's the biggest and the best,
though it might not be the cheapest.
How much is it—more than all the rest?
I'll pass on some good advice to you:
When you're in Rome, do as the Romans do.
A ten percent tip for the taxi fare
should be good enough when you're staying
there.

(CHORUS)